Working Papers

FINANCIAL ACCOUNTING

Working Papers

FINANCIAL ACCOUNTING

Jane L. Reimers

Albert Fisher

Community College of Southern Nevada

PEARSON

Prentice
Hall

Upper Saddle River, New Jersey 07458

VP/Editorial Director: Jeff Shelstad
Acquisitions Editor: Steve Sartori
Associate Editor: Joanna Doxey
Associate Director Manufacturing: Vincent Scelta
Production Editor & Buyer: Wanda Rockwell
Printer/Binder: Bind-Rite Graphics

10 9 8 7 6 5 4 3 2 1
ISBN 0-13-186766-0

Table of Contents

Question 1

_____

_____

_____

_____

_____

Question 2

_____

_____

_____

_____

Question 3

_____

_____

_____

_____

Question 4

_____

_____

_____

_____

Question 5

_____

_____

_____

_____

_____

_____

Question 6

Question 7

Question 8

Question 9

Question 10

Name _____

Section _____

Question 11

_____

_____

_____

_____

_____

Question 12

_____

_____

_____

_____

Question 13

_____

_____

_____

_____

Question 14

_____

_____

_____

_____

Multiple choice: _____

1. _____   6. _____
2. _____   7. _____
3. _____   8. _____
4. _____   9. _____
5. _____   10. _____

SE1-1 _____

_____

_____

_____

_____

SE1-2 a. _____

b. _____

c. _____

d. _____

e. _____

SE1-3 _____

_____

_____

_____

_____

SE1-4 a. _____

b. _____

c. _____

d. _____

e. _____

f. _____

SE1-5 _____

_____

_____

_____

_____

_____

_____

_____

SE1-6

_____
_____
_____
_____
_____

SE1-7

	Revenues	- Expenses	=	Net Income
	560	- 350		
		- 475		500
	940	- 600		
	1,240	-		670
		- 2,500		6,450

SE1-8

	Assets	= Liabilities	+	Owner's Equity
	125,000	= 35,750	+	

SE1-9

	Assets	= Liabilities	+	Owner's Equity
	75,000	= 20,000	+	

SE1-10

	Assets	= Liabilities	+	Owner's Equity
		=	+	

SE1-11

	Assets	= Liabilities	+	Contributed Capital	Retained Earnings
	6,000	= 3,000	+	1,000	+

_____
_____
_____
_____

SE1-12

_____

_____

_____

_____

SE1-13

_____

_____

_____

_____

SE1-14	Type of account	Financial Statement
a. Interest expense		
b. Accounts receivable		
c. Equipment		
d. Paid-in capital		
e. Sales revenue		

SE1-15

_____

_____

_____

_____

_____

_____

E1-1A

a. Assets

b. Liabilities

c.

Name _____

Section _____

E1-2A

a. _____

b. _____

c. _____

d. _____

e. _____

f. _____

E1-3A

a. _____

b. _____

c. _____

d. _____

e. _____

f. _____

g. _____

E1-4A

a. _____

b. _____

c. _____

d. _____

e. _____

f. _____

g. _____

E1-5A

a. _____

b. _____

c. _____

d. _____

e. _____

_____

_____

_____

E1-10A

a. _____

b. _____

c. _____

d. _____

e. _____

f. _____

g. _____

E1-11A

	Dec. 31 2006	Dec. 31 2007
Assets	1,000	2,500
Liabilities	x	1,000
Contributed capital	300	300
Retained earnings	Y	z
Revenue	300	2,500
Expenses	100	1,500

E1-12A

	Type of account	Financial Statement
a. Interest revenue		
b. Accounts payable		
c. Land		
d. Cash		
e. Common stock		
f. Retained earnings		
g. Rent expense		
h. Total stockholders' equity		
i. Total assets		
j. Net income		
k. Operating expenses		
l. Total operating expenses		
m. Cash generated by operating activities		

E1-13A

E1-14A

a.

b.

c.

d.

E1-1B

a. Assets

b. Liabilities

c.

E1-2B

a. _____

b. _____

c. _____

d. _____

e. _____

f. _____

E1-3B

a. _____

b. _____

c. _____

d. _____

e. _____

f. _____

g. _____

E1-4B

a. _____

b. _____

c. _____

d. _____

e. _____

f. _____

g. _____

E1-5B

a. _____

b. _____

c. _____

d. _____

e. _____

E1-6B

a. _____

b. _____

c. _____

d. _____

E1-7B

a. _____

b. _____

c. _____

d. _____

e. _____

f. _____

E1-8B

a. _____

b. _____

c. _____

d. _____

e. _____

f. _____

E1-9B

a. _____

b. _____

c. _____

d. _____

e. _____

f. _____

g. _____

h. _____

_____

_____

_____

_____

E1-10B

a.

b.

c.

d.

e.

f.

g.

E1-11B

	June 30 2009	June 30 2010
Assets	2,000	3,700
Liabilities	x	2,500
Contributed capital	500	700
Retained earnings	y	z
Revenue	800	7,200
Expenses	250	6,700

E1-12B

	Type of account	Financial Statement
a. Sales revenue		
b. Notes payable		
c. Equipment		
d. Accounts receivable		
e. Common stock		
f. Retained earnings		
g. Interest expense		
h. Total stockholders' equity		
i. Total liabilities		
j. Net loss		
k. Salaries expense		
l. Total assets		
m. Cash generated by operating activities		

E1-13B

E1-14B

a.

b.

c.

d.

Name _____
Section _____

Problem 1-1A

Assets =	Liabilities +	Contributed Capital +	Retained Earnings

a. _____

_____

b. _____

_____

c. _____

_____

d. _____

_____

e. _____

_____

_____

Name _____

Section _____

Problem 1-2A

a. 1. _____

2. _____

3. _____

4. _____

5. _____

_____

b. _____

_____

_____

_____

_____

_____

c. _____

_____

_____

_____

_____

_____

_____

_____

_____

_____

_____

_____

_____

_____

_____

_____

Problem 1-3A

Transaction	Operating (O), Investing (I), or Financing (F)	Effect on Assets	Effect on Net Income	Financial Statement
1				
2				
3				
4				
5				
6				
7				
8				
9				
10				

Problem 1-4A

a. _____

_____

_____

_____

_____

_____

_____

_____

_____

b. _____

_____

_____

_____

c. _____

_____

_____

_____

d. _____

_____

_____

_____

_____

_____

_____

_____

_____

Problem 1-3B

_____

_____

Transaction	Operating (O), Investing (I), or Financing (F)	Effect on Assets	Effect on Net Income	Financial Statement
1				
2				
3				
4				
5				
6				
7				
8				
9				
10				

_____

_____

_____

_____

_____

_____

_____

_____

_____

_____

_____

Name _____

Section _____

Problem 1-4B

a.

b.

c.

d.

Financial Statement Analysis Problems

1-1   a.

1-2   a.

1-3   a.

Name _____

Section _____

Critical Thinking Problems

Question 6

_____

_____

_____

_____

Question 7

_____

_____

_____

_____

Question 8

_____

_____

_____

_____

Question 9

_____

_____

_____

Question 10

_____

_____

_____

_____

_____

_____

Question 11

_____

_____

_____

_____

Question 12

_____

_____

_____

_____

Question 13

_____

_____

_____

_____

Question 14

_____

_____

_____

_____

Question 15

_____

_____

Question 16

_____

_____

_____

_____

Question 17

_____

_____

_____

_____

_____

Question 18

_____

_____

_____

_____

Question 19

_____

_____

_____

_____

Question 20

_____

_____

_____

_____

_____

Multiple choice: _____

1. _____	6. _____
2. _____	7. _____
3. _____	8. _____
4. _____	9. _____
5. _____	10. _____

SE2-1

	Income Statement	Balance Sheet

SE2-2

		Financial Statement(s)
	Cash	
	Sales revenue	
	Cost of goods sold	
	Equipment	
	Long-Term Debt	
	Contributed capital	
	Accounts Receivable	
	Cash from operations	
	Retained earnings	
	Net income	

SE2-3	a.	SE2-6	a.
	b.		b.
	c.		c.
			d.
SE2-4	a.		e.
	b.		f.
	c.		
	d.		

SE2-5	a.
	b.
	c.
	d.

SE2-13   Type of account

    a. Furniture and fixtures

    b. Cash

    c. Short-term investments

    d. Property and equipment

    e. Supplies

    f. Prepaid insurance

    g. Accounts receivable

SE2-14

    a.

    b.

    c.

SE2-15

SE2-16

The Accounting Equation

Assets	=	Liabilities	+	Shareholders' Equity	
				Contributed capital	+	Retained earnings

a.

b.

c.

d.

e.

SE2-17

a.

b.

c.

d.

SE2-18

a.

b.

c.

SE2-19

E2-1A

E2-2A   Financial Statement

Cash

Accounts payable

Revenue

Cash from investing activities

Land

Common stock

Accounts receivable

Prepaid insurance

Insurance expense

Operating expenses

Cash from financing activities

E2-3A

E2-4A

E2-5A

E2-6A

		F/S and account type
Equipment	$ 231,300	
Accounts receivable	45,600	
Prepaid insurance	6,700	
Cash	57,890	
Short-term notes payable	23,200	
Cash from investing activities	89,300	
Land	45,200	
Common stock	100,000	
Retained earnings	75,000	
Cash from financing activities	45,980	
Accounts payable	32,100	
Long-term mortgage payable	54,000	
Interest payable	2,500	
Cash from operating activities	34,350	

E2-7A

		Account type
Salaries payable	$ 3,607	
Equipment	14,280	
Accounts payable	3,660	
Long-term note payable	2,000	
Common stock	15,000	
Cash	35,879	
Accounts receivable	14,250	
Interest receivable	1,000	
Retained earnings	25,200	

E2-8A

E2-8A (continued)

E2-8A (continued)

Name _____
Section _____

E2-9A

The Accounting Equation

	Assets	=	Liabilities	+	Shareholders' Equity	
					Contributed capital	+	Retained earnings
a.						
b.						
c.						
d.						

E2-10A

The Accounting Equation

	Assets	=	Liabilities	+	Shareholders' Equity	
					Contributed capital	+	Retained earnings
a.						
b.						
c.						
d.						
e.						
f.						

E2-11A

E2-5B

E2-6B

		F/S and account type
Van	$ 50,500	
Interest receivable	32,500	
Prepaid rent	5,425	
Cash	78,000	
Short-term loan payable	15,875	
Cash from operating activities	28,000	
Building	31,853	
Common stock	75,000	
Retained earnings	100,000	
Cash from investing activities	40,000	
Interest payable	650	
Long-term mortgage payable	85,000	
Salaries payable	1,315	
Cash from financing activities	10,000	

E2-7B

		Account type
Accounts payable	$ 1,385	
Computer	2,525	
Interest payable	3,521	
Long-term note payable	1,875	
Common stock	3,815	
Prepaid rent	1,975	
Short-term loan receivable	10,375	
Interest receivable	1,520	
Retained earnings	16,785	

Name _____

Section _____

E2-11B

The Accounting Equation

	Assets	=	Liabilities	+	Shareholders' Equity	
					Contributed capital	+	Retained earnings
a.						
b.						
c.						
d.						
e.						

E2-11B (continued)

P2-2A

Part a.

Part b.

P2-3A

Part a.

Part b.

P2-5A

Part b.

Part c.

The Accounting Equation

Assets	=	Liabilities	+	Shareholders' Equity	
				Contributed capital	+	Retained earnings

P2-6A (continued)

Part b.

Part c.

P2-7A

Part a.

_____

_____

_____

_____

_____

_____

_____

_____

_____

_____

Part b.

_____

_____

_____

_____

Part c.

P2-7A (continued)

Part d.

Part e.

P2-7A (continued)

Part f.

Part g.

P2-9A (continued)

Part b.

Part c. _____

_____

_____

Part d. _____

_____

_____

_____

P2-1B

Name _____

Section _____

Part a.

Part b.

Chapter 2

Name ________________

P2-5B

Section ________________

Part b.

Part c.

Name _____

Section _____

The Accounting Equation

Assets	=	Liabilities	+	Shareholders' Equity	
				Contributed capital	+	Retained earnings

P2-8B

Part a.

_____
_____
_____
_____
_____
_____
_____
_____
_____
_____
_____
_____

Part b.

_____
_____
_____
_____
_____

Part c.

P2-8B (continued)

Part d.		

Part e.		

P2-9B (continued)

Part b.

Part c.

Part d.

Name _____

Section _____

Financial Statement Analysis Problems

2-1

2-2

2-3

Name _____
Section _____

Question 11

_____

_____

_____

_____

_____

Question 12

_____

_____

_____

_____

_____

Question 13

_____

_____

_____

_____

_____

Question 14

_____

_____

_____

_____

_____

Multiple choice: _____

1. _____   6. _____
2. _____   7. _____
3. _____   8. _____
4. _____   9. _____
5. _____   10. _____

SE3-1

Account title	Revenue	Expense	Asset	Liability
a. Sales revenue				
b. Service revenue				
c. Accounts receivable				
d. Utilities expense				
e. Salary expense				
f. Accounts payable				
g. Interest expense				

SE3-2

Date	Journal Entry	Debit	Credit

SE3-3

	Account Credited
a. Issued stock for cash.	
b. Borrowed money from bank.	
c. Provided services to customers for cash.	
d. Provided services to customers on account.	

SE3-14

_____

_____

_____

_____

SE3-15

_____

_____

_____

_____

_____

_____

SE3-16

_____

_____

_____

_____

_____

SE3-17

_____

_____

_____

_____

_____

_____

Name _____

Section _____

E3-1A

General Journal

Date	Accounts and Explanations	Post. Ref.	Debit	Credit

Name _____
Section _____

E3-3A

Cash

E3-4A

General Journal

Date	Accounts and Explanations	Post. Ref.	Debit	Credit

E3-4A (continued)

Cash

E3-4A (continued)

E3-5A

Cash

E3-5A (continued)

E3-6A

E3-7A

E3-7A (continued)

E3-10A (continued)

Cash

Name _____

Section _____

E3-11A

E3-11A (continued)

Name _____

Section _____

E3-12A

a.

b.

c.

d.

e.

f.

g.

h.

i.

E3-13A

E3-14A

E3-15A

Accounts Payable

E3-16A

Land

P3-1A

General Journal

Part a.

Date	Accounts and Explanations	Post. Ref.	Debit	Credit

P3-1A (continued) Part b.

Cash

P3-1A (continued)

Part c.

P3-2A

General Journal

Part a.

Date	Accounts and Explanations	Post. Ref.	Debit	Credit

P3-2A (continued) Part b.

Cash

P3-2A (continued)

Part c.		

Part d.		

Name _____

Section _____

P3-2A (continued)

Part d.

Part d.

P3-2A (continued)

Part d.		

P3-3A

Part a.

Name _____
Section _____

P3-3A (continued) Part b.

Cash

P3-3A (continued)

Part b.		

Part c.		

P3-3A (continued)

Part c.

Part c.

Name _____

Section _____

P3-3A (continued)

Part c.		

P3-3A (continued)

Part d.

P3-4A

Part a.		

Part c.		

Name _____

Section _____

P3-4A (continued) Part b.

Cash

Name _____
Section _____

P3-5A Part a.

Cash

P3-5A (continued)

General Journal

Part b.

Date	Accounts and Explanations	Post. Ref.	Debit	Credit

P3-5A (continued)

Part c.		

Part d.		

Name _____

Section _____

P3-5A (continued)

Part e.

Name _____

Section _____

P3-6A

General Journal

Part a.

Date	Accounts and Explanations	Post. Ref.	Debit	Credit

P3-6A (continued) Part b.

Cash

P3-6A (continued)

Part c.		

Part d.		

P3-6A (continued)

Part d.

Part d.

P3-6A (continued)

Part d.

P3-7A

Part a.

_____

_____

_____

_____

_____

_____

_____

Part b.

Cash

P3-7A (continued)

Part b.		

Part c.

P3-8A

Part a.

Accounts Receivable

Part b.

Accounts Payable

Part c.

Salaries Payable

Part d.

Interest Receivable

P3-1B

General Journal

Part a.

Date	Accounts and Explanations	Post. Ref.	Debit	Credit

P3-1B (continued) Part b.

Cash

P3-1B (continued)

Part c.		

Name _____

Section _____

P3-2B

General Journal

Part a.

Date	Accounts and Explanations	Post. Ref.	Debit	Credit

P3-2B (continued) Part b.

Cash

Name _____

Section _____

P3-2B (continued)

Part c.

Part d.

Name _____

Section _____

P3-2B (continued)

Part d.		

Part d.		

P3-2B (continued)

Part d.		

Name _____

Section _____

P3-3B

Part a.

P3-3B (continued) Part b.

Cash

Name _____

Section _____

P3-3B (continued)

Part b.		

Part c.		

P3-3B (continued)

Part c.

Part c.

P3-3B (continued)

Part c.		

P3-3B (continued)

Part d.

P3-4B

Part a.		

Part c.		

P3-4B (continued) Part b.

Cash

Name _____

Section _____

P3-5B Part a.

Cash

P3-5B

General Journal

Part b.

Date	Accounts and Explanations	Post. Ref.	Debit	Credit

P3-5B (continued)

Part c.		

Part d.		

Name ______________

Section ______________

P3-5B (continued)

Part d.

Part d.

P3-5B (continued)

Part d.		

P3-5B (continued)

Part e.

P3-6B

General Journal

Part a.

Date	Accounts and Explanations	Post. Ref.	Debit	Credit

Name _____

Section _____

P3-6B (continued) Part b.

Cash

P3-6B (continued)

Part c.

Part d.

P3-6B (continued)

Part d.

Part d.

P3-6B (continued)

Part d.		

P3-8B

Part a.

Accounts Receivable

Part b.

Accounts Payable

Part c.

Salaries Payable

Part d.

Interest Receivable

Financial Statement Analysis Problems

3-1

3-2

Name _____

Section _____

Financial Statement Analysis Problems

3-3

Name _____

Section _____

Critical Thinking Problems

Name _____

Section _____

Internet Exercises

3-1

3-2

3-3

Chapter 4

Name ____________________

Section ________

Question 1

Question 2

Question 3

Question 4

Question 5

Question 6

_____

_____

_____

_____

Question 7

_____

_____

_____

_____

Question 8

_____

_____

_____

_____

Question 9

_____

_____

_____

_____

Question 10

_____

_____

_____

_____

_____

_____

Question 11

_____

_____

_____

_____

_____

Question 12

_____

_____

_____

_____

_____

Question 13

_____

_____

_____

_____

_____

Question 14

_____

_____

_____

_____

Question 15

_____

_____

_____

_____

_____

_____

SE4-5

_____

_____

_____

_____

_____

_____

SE4-6

_____

_____

_____

_____

_____

_____

SE4-7

_____

_____

_____

_____

_____

_____

SE4-8

_____

_____

_____

_____

_____

_____

SE4-9

_____

_____

_____

_____

_____

_____

SE4-10

Cash

Accounts receivable

Prepaid insurance

Supplies

Building

Accumulated depreciation

Unearned revenue

Interest payable

Salaries payable

Common stock

Retained earnings

Sales revenue

Interest revenue

Depreciation expense

Insurance expense

Supplies expense

Utilities expense

Rent expense

SE4-11

SE4-11 (continued)

E4-1A

_____
_____
_____
_____
_____
_____
_____

E4-2A

_____
_____
_____
_____
_____
_____
_____

E4-3A	Interest Expense	Cash Paid for Interest
November 30, 2006		
December 31, 2006		
January 31, 2007		

E4-4A	General Journal	Debit	Credit

_____
_____
_____
_____
_____
_____
_____

E4-5A	Rent Expense for the Year	Prepaid Rent at December 31
2008		
2009		

E4-6A	Revenue Recognized	Unearned Revenue at December 31
2009		
2010		
2011		
2012		

E4-7A	Insurance Expense	Prepaid Insurance at December 31
2008		
2009		
2010		

E4-8A

E4-9A

General Journal

Date	Accounts and Explanations	Post. Ref.	Debit	Credit

E4-10A

General Journal

Date	Accounts and Explanations	Post. Ref.	Debit	Credit

E4-11A

E4-12A

General Journal	Debit	Credit

E4-12A (continued)

Chapter 4

Name ____________
Section ____________

E4-13A

General Journal	Debit	Credit

E4-13A (continued)

E4-14A

Interest receivable _____

Salary expense _____

Notes receivable _____

Unearned revenue _____

Cash flow from investing activities _____

Insurance expense _____

Retained earnings _____

Prepaid insurance _____

Cash _____

Accumulated depreciation _____

Prepaid rent _____

Accounts receivable _____

Total shareholders' equity _____

Accounts payable _____

Common stock _____

Dividends _____

Total assets _____

Net income _____

Consulting revenue _____

Depreciation expense _____

Supplies expense _____

Salaries payable _____

Supplies _____

Cash flow from financing activities _____

Land _____

Cash flow from operating activities _____

Name _____

Section _____

E4-15A

E4-16A

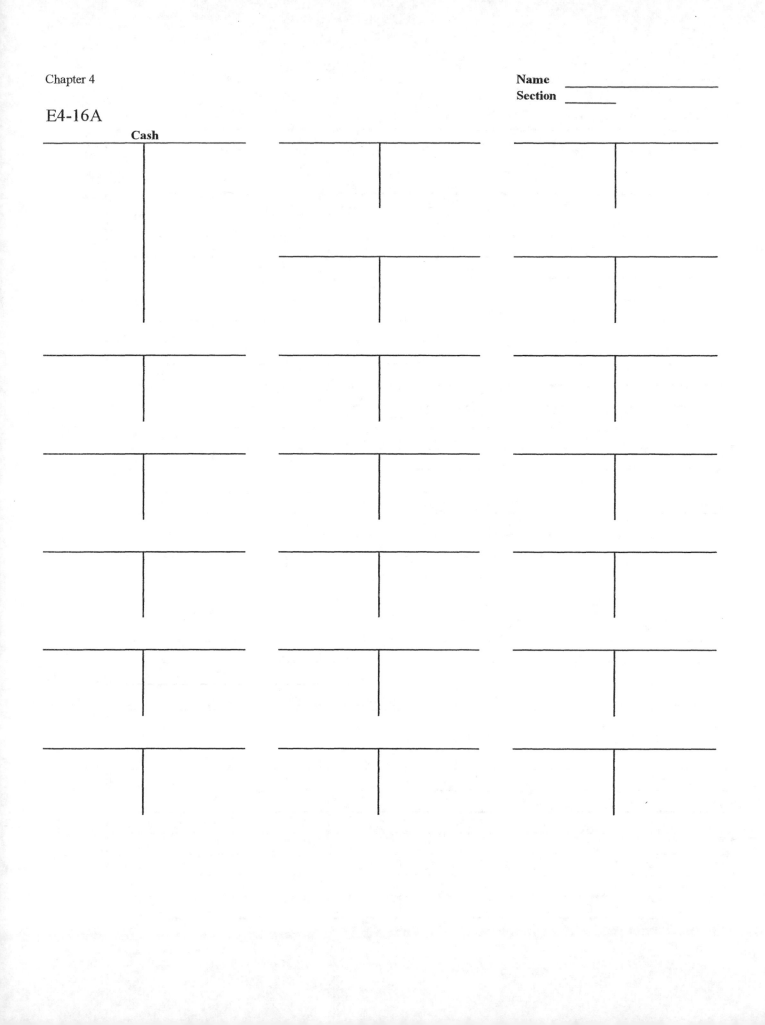

Cash

E4-16A (continued)

E4-16A (continued)

E4-16A (continued)

General Journal	Debit	Credit

E4-17A

E4-1B

_____

_____

_____

_____

_____

_____

E4-2B

_____

_____

_____

_____

_____

E4-3B	Interest Expense	Cash Paid for Interest
January 31, 2008		
February 29, 2008		
March 31. 2008		
April 30, 2008		

E4-4B	General Journal	Debit	Credit

_____

_____

_____

_____

_____

E4-5B	Rent Expense for the Year	Prepaid Rent at December 31
2006		
2007		
2008		

E4-6B	Revenue Recognized	Unearned Revenue at June 30
2010		
2011		
2012		

E4-7B	Insurance Expense	Prepaid Insurance at December 31
2009		
2010		
2011		

E4-8B

E4-9B

General Journal

Date	Accounts and Explanations	Post. Ref.	Debit	Credit

E4-10B

General Journal

Date	Accounts and Explanations	Post. Ref.	Debit	Credit

_____

_____

_____

_____

_____

_____

_____

E4-11B

_____

_____

_____

E4-12B

General Journal	Debit	Credit

E4-12B (continued)

E4-13B

General Journal	Debit	Credit

E4-13B (continued)

E4-14B

Cash

Accounts receivable

Prepaid insurance

Prepaid rent

Supplies

Depreciation expense

Insurance expense

Supplies expense

Utilities expense

Rent expense

Interest receivable

Common stock

Retained earnings

Sales revenue

Interest revenue

Equipment

Accumulated depreciation—equipment

Unearned revenue

Interest payable

Salaries payable

Accounts payable

Other operating expense

Name _____

Section _____

E4-15B _____

Chapter 4

Name _____
Section _____

E4-16B

Cash

E4-16B (continued)

P4-1A

General Journal

Part a.

Date	Accounts and Explanations	Post. Ref.	Debit	Credit

Name _____

Section _____

P4-1A (continued) Part b.

P4-2A

General Journal

Part a.

Date	Accounts and Explanations	Post. Ref.	Debit	Credit

P4-2A (continued) Part b.

P4-3A

General Journal

Part a.

Date	Accounts and Explanations	Post. Ref.	Debit	Credit

Part b.

_____

_____

_____

_____

_____

_____

Part c.

_____

_____

_____

_____

_____

Part d.

P4-4A

General Journal

Part a.

Date	Accounts and Explanations	Post. Ref.	Debit	Credit

P4-4A (continued) Part b.

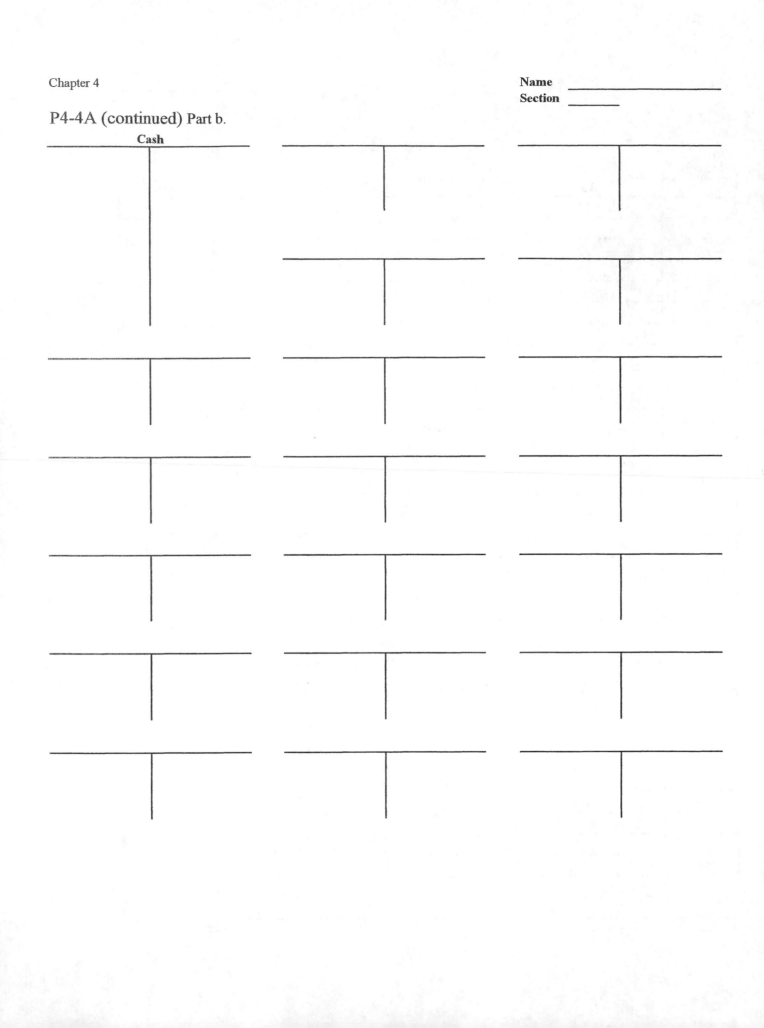

Cash

P4-4A (continued) Part c.

Prepaid Insurance

Prepaid Rent

Interest Receivable

Salaries Payable

Unearned Fee Income

Interest Income

Fees

Rent Expense

Insurance Expense

Salaries Expense

Name _____

Section _____

P4-5A

General Journal

Part a.

Date	Accounts and Explanations	Post. Ref.	Debit	Credit

Name _____

Section _____

P4-5A (continued) Part b.

Cash

P4-5A (continued) Part c.

Prepaid Insurance

Prepaid Rent

Wages Payable

Interest Payable

Wages Expense

Subscription Income

Unearned Sub. Income

Interest Expense

Rent Expense

Insurance Expense

P4-6A Parts a and b.

Part c.

Prepaid Insurance	
Revenue	
Wages Expense	
Taxes Payable	
Interest Income	
Interest Receivable	
Wages Payable	
Unearned Revenue	
Insurance Expense	

Part d.

P4-7A Parts a and c.

Cash

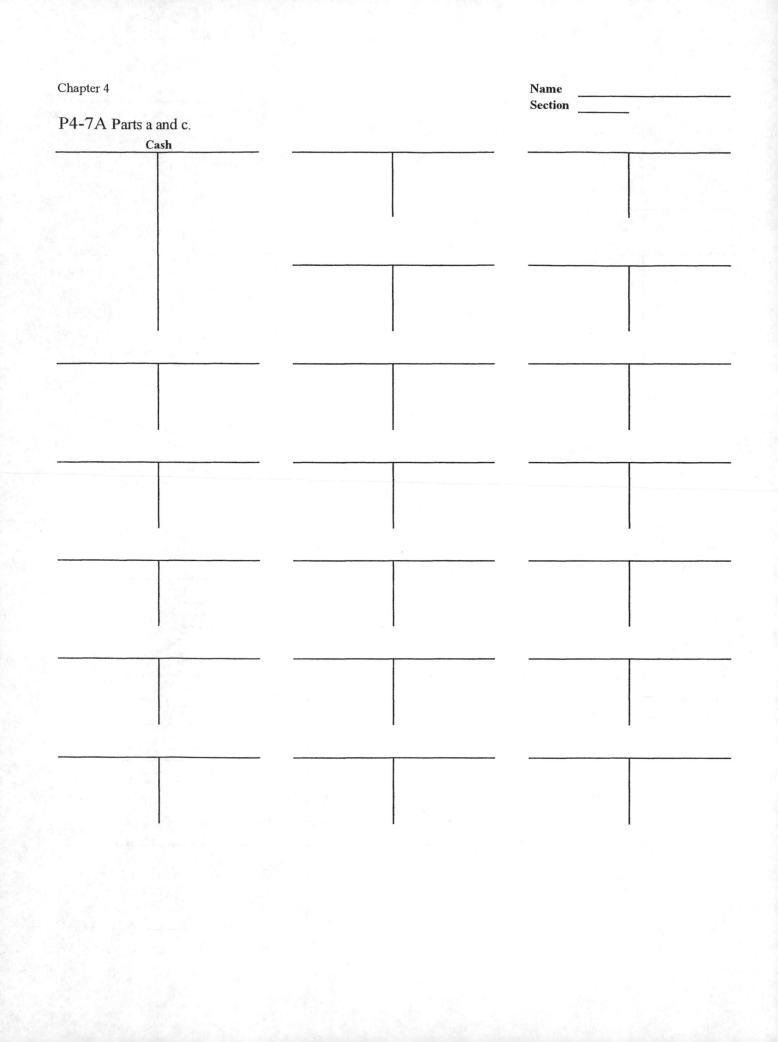

Name _____

Section _____

P4-7A (continued)

General Journal

Part b.

Date	Accounts and Explanations	Post. Ref.	Debit	Credit

Name _____

Section _____

P4-7A (continued)

General Journal

Part b.

Date	Accounts and Explanations	Post. Ref.	Debit	Credit

P4-7A (continued) Part d.

P4-7A (continued) Part d.

P4-7A (continued) Part d.

P4-7A (continued)

General Journal

Part e.

Date	Accounts and Explanations	Post. Ref.	Debit	Credit

P4-8A

General Journal

Part a.

Date	Accounts and Explanations	Post. Ref.	Debit	Credit

P4-8A (continued) Parts b and c.

Cash

P4-8A (continued) Part d.

P4-8A (continued) Part d.

P4-8A (continued) Part d.

P4-8A (continued)

General Journal

Part e.

Date	Accounts and Explanations	Post. Ref.	Debit	Credit

P4-9A

General Journal

Part a.

Date	Accounts and Explanations	Post. Ref.	Debit	Credit

P4-9A (continued) Part b.

Cash

P4-9A (continued) Part c.

P4-9A (continued) Part c.

P4-9A (continued) Part c.

P4-9A (continued)

General Journal

Part d.

Date	Accounts and Explanations	Post. Ref.	Debit	Credit

P4-10A Part a.

Cash

P4-10A (continued) Part b.

Account	Debit	Credit

P4-10A (continued) Part c.

P4-10A (continued) Part c.

P4-10A (continued)

General Journal

Part d.

Date	Accounts and Explanations	Post. Ref.	Debit	Credit

P4-10A (continued) Part e.

Account	Debit	Credit

Name _____

Section _____

P4-11A, Part a.

_____

_____

_____

_____

_____

_____

_____

_____

_____

_____

_____

_____

_____

_____

_____

_____

_____

_____

_____

_____

_____

_____

_____

_____

_____

_____

_____

_____

_____

_____

P4-11A (continued) Part b.

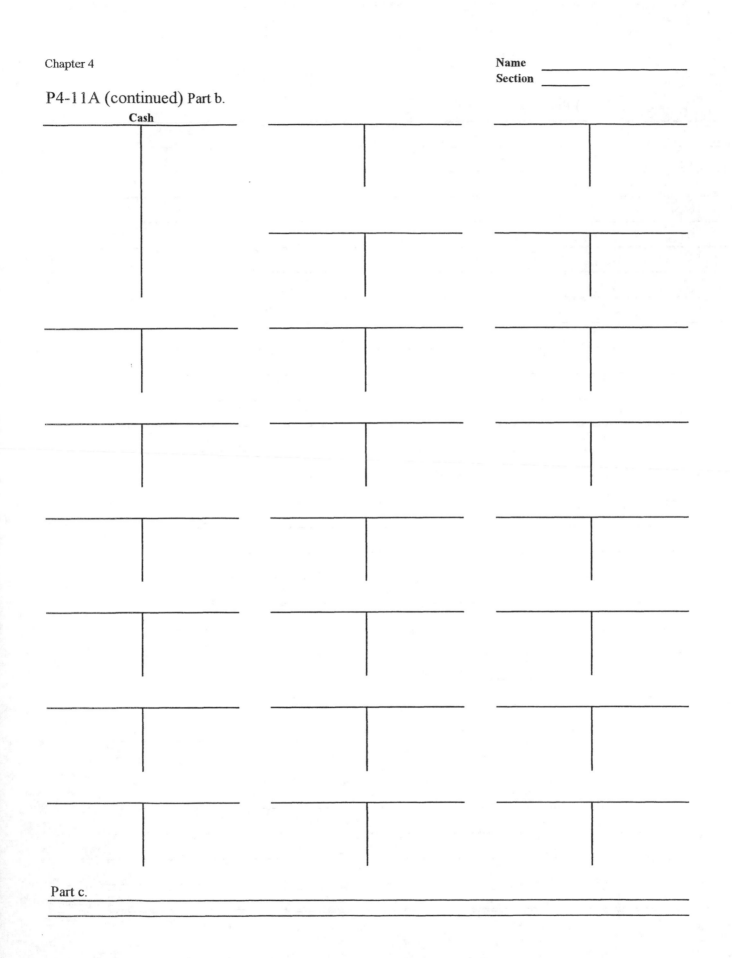

Cash

Part c.

P4-11A (continued) Part d.

P4-11A (continued) Part d.

P4-11A (continued) Part d.

P4-11A (continued)

General Journal

Part e.

Date	Accounts and Explanations	Post. Ref.	Debit	Credit

P4-1B

General Journal

Part a.

Date	Accounts and Explanations	Post. Ref.	Debit	Credit

Name _____

Section _____

P4-1B (continued) Part b.

P4-2B Part a.

Cash

P4-2B (continued) Part b.

P4-3B

General Journal

Part a.

Date	Accounts and Explanations	Post. Ref.	Debit	Credit

Part b.

_____

_____

_____

_____

_____

_____

_____

_____

Part c.

_____

_____

_____

_____

_____

_____

Part d.

P4-4B

General Journal

Part a.

Date	Accounts and Explanations	Post. Ref.	Debit	Credit

Name _____
Section _____

P4-4B (continued) Part b.

Cash

P4-4B (continued) Part c.

Prepaid Rent

Prepaid Insurance

Interest Payable

Wages Payable

Unearned Service Revenue

Service Revenue

Interest Expense

Rent Expense

Insurance Expense

Wage Expense

P4-5B

General Journal

Part a.

Date	Accounts and Explanations	Post. Ref.	Debit	Credit

Name _____
Section _____

P4-5B (continued) Part b.

Cash

Name _____

Section _____

P4-5B (continued) Part c.

Prepaid Insurance

Prepaid Rent

Interest Payable

Wages Payable

Wage Expense

Unearned Subscription Revenue

Subscription Revenue

Interest Expense

Insurance Expense

Rent Expense

P4-6B Parts a and b.

Part c.

Prepaid Insurance

Interest Receivable

Desks (Inventory)

Wages Payable

Accounts Payable

Unearned Rental Revenue

Rental Income

Wages Expense

Insurance Expense

Interest Revenue

Part d.

P4-7B Parts a and c.

Cash

P4-7B Parts a and c.

P4-7B (continued)

General Journal

Part b.

Date	Accounts and Explanations	Post. Ref.	Debit	Credit

P4-7B (continued)

General Journal

Part b.

Date	Accounts and Explanations	Post. Ref.	Debit	Credit

P4-7B (continued) Part d.

P4-7B (continued) Part d.

P4-7B (continued) Part d.

P4-7B (continued)

General Journal

Part e.

Date	Accounts and Explanations	Post. Ref.	Debit	Credit

P4-8B

General Journal

Part a.

Date	Accounts and Explanations	Post. Ref.	Debit	Credit

P4-8B (continued) Parts b and c.

Cash

P4-8B (continued) Part d.

P4-8B (continued) Part d.

P4-8B (continued) Part d.

P4-8B (continued)

General Journal

Part e.

Date	Accounts and Explanations	Post. Ref.	Debit	Credit

Name _____

Section _____

P4-9B

General Journal

Part a.

Date	Accounts and Explanations	Post. Ref.	Debit	Credit

P4-9B (continued) Part b.

Cash

P4-9B (continued) Part c.

P4-9B (continued) Part c.

P4-9B (continued) Part c.

P4-9B (continued)

General Journal

Part d.

Date	Accounts and Explanations	Post. Ref.	Debit	Credit

P4-10B Part a.

Cash

P4-10B Part a.

P4-10B (continued) Part b.

Account	Debit	Credit

P4-10B (continued) Part c.

P4-10A (continued), part c.

P4-10B (continued)

General Journal

Part d.

Date	Accounts and Explanations	Post. Ref.	Debit	Credit

P4-10B (continued) Part e.

Account	Debit	Credit

Name _____

Section _____

P4-11B Part 1.

P4-11B (continued) Part 2.

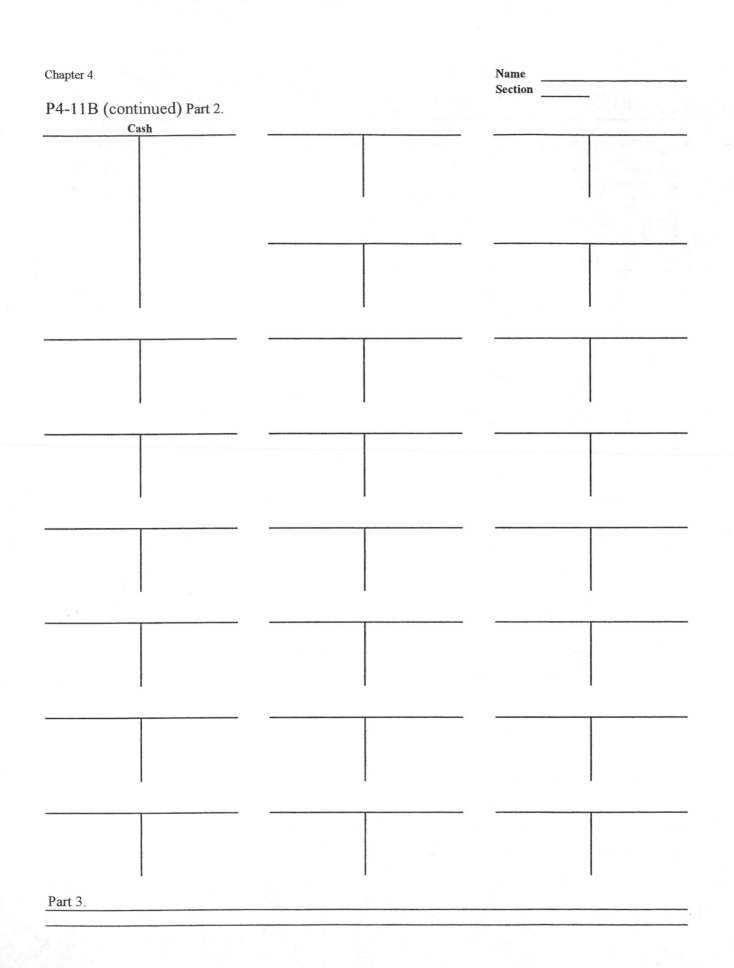

Cash

Part 3. _____

P4-11B (continued) Part 4.

P4-11B (continued) Part 4.

P4-11B (continued) Part 4.

P4-1B (continued) Part b.

P4-2B Part a.

Cash

P4-2B (continued) Part b.

P4-3B

General Journal

Part a.

Date	Accounts and Explanations	Post. Ref.	Debit	Credit

Part b.

_____

_____

_____

_____

_____

_____

_____

Part c.

_____

_____

_____

_____

_____

Part d.

Name _____

Section _____

P4-4B

General Journal

Part a.

Date	Accounts and Explanations	Post. Ref.	Debit	Credit

P4-4B (continued) Part b.

Cash

P4-4B (continued) Part c.

Prepaid Rent _____

Prepaid Insurance _____

Interest Payable _____

Wages Payable _____

Unearned Service Revenue _____

Service Revenue _____

Interest Expense _____

Rent Expense _____

Insurance Expense _____

Wage Expense _____

_____

_____

_____

_____

_____

_____

_____

_____

_____

_____

_____

_____

_____

_____

_____

_____

_____

_____

P4-5B

General Journal

Part a.

Date	Accounts and Explanations	Post. Ref.	Debit	Credit

Name _____
Section _____

P4-5B (continued) Part b.

Cash

P4-5B (continued) Part c.

Prepaid Insurance

Prepaid Rent

Interest Payable

Wages Payable

Wage Expense

Unearned Subscription Revenue

Subscription Revenue

Interest Expense

Insurance Expense

Rent Expense

Chapter 4

P4-6B Parts a and b.

Part c.

Prepaid Insurance

Interest Receivable

Desks (Inventory)

Wages Payable

Accounts Payable

Unearned Rental Revenue

Rental Income

Wages Expense

Insurance Expense

Interest Revenue

Part d.

Name _____
Section _____

P4-7B Parts a and c.

Cash

P4-7B Parts a and c.

P4-7B (continued)

General Journal

Part b.

Date	Accounts and Explanations	Post. Ref.	Debit	Credit

P4-7B (continued)

General Journal

Part b.

Date	Accounts and Explanations	Post. Ref.	Debit	Credit

P4-7B (continued) Part d.

P4-7B (continued) Part d.

P4-7B (continued) Part d.

P4-7B (continued)

General Journal

Part e.

Date	Accounts and Explanations	Post. Ref.	Debit	Credit

Name _____

Section _____

P4-8B

General Journal

Part a.

Date	Accounts and Explanations	Post. Ref.	Debit	Credit

P4-8B (continued) Parts b and c.

Cash

P4-8B (continued) Part d.

P4-8B (continued) Part d.

P4-8B (continued) Part d.

P4-8B (continued)

General Journal

Part e.

Date	Accounts and Explanations	Post. Ref.	Debit	Credit

P4-9B

General Journal

Part a.

Date	Accounts and Explanations	Post. Ref.	Debit	Credit

P4-9B (continued) Part b.

Cash

P4-9B (continued) Part c.

P4-9B (continued) Part c.

P4-9B (continued) Part c.

P4-9B (continued)

General Journal

Part d.

Date	Accounts and Explanations	Post. Ref.	Debit	Credit

P4-10B Part a.

Cash

P4-10B Part a.

(blank T-accounts)

P4-10B (continued) Part b.

Account	Debit	Credit

Name _____

Section _____

P4-10B (continued) Part c.

P4-10A (continued), part c.

P4-10B (continued)

General Journal

Part d.

Date	Accounts and Explanations	Post. Ref.	Debit	Credit

P4-10B (continued) Part e.

Account	Debit	Credit

Name _____

Section _____

P4-11B Part 1.

P4-11B (continued) Part 2.

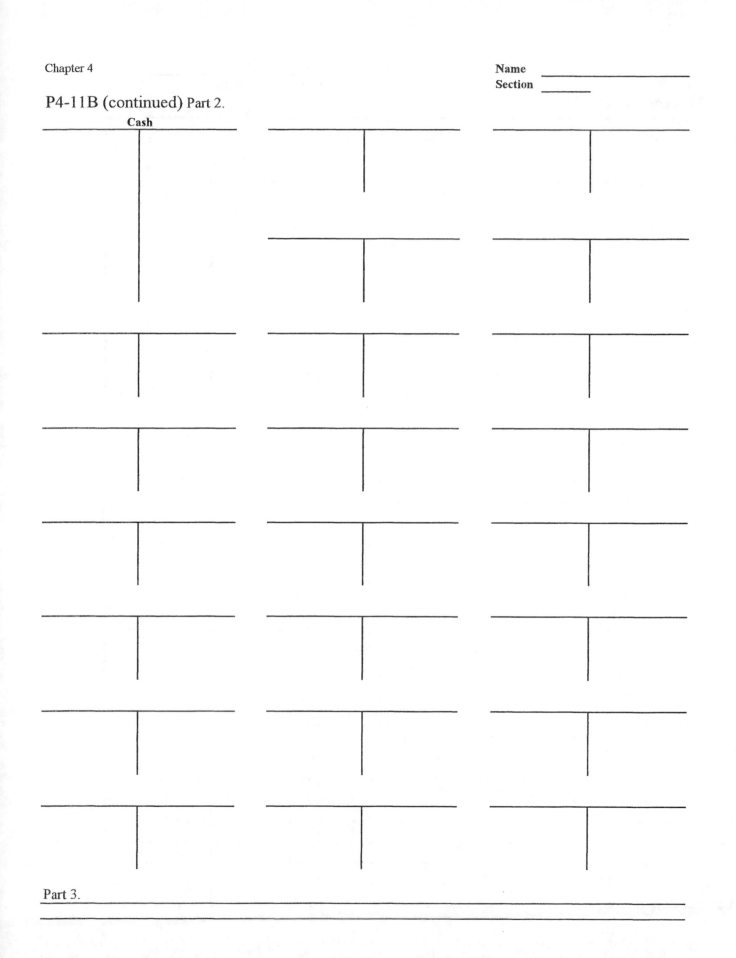

Cash

Part 3.

P4-11B (continued) Part 4.

P4-11B (continued) Part 4.

Name _____

Section _____

P4-11B (continued) Part 4.

P4-11B (continued)

General Journal

Part 5.

Date	Accounts and Explanations	Post. Ref.	Debit	Credit

Name _____

Section _____

Financial Statement Analysis Problems

4-1

4-2

4-3

Financial Statement Analysis Problems

4-4

4-5

Name _____

Section _____

Critical Thinking Problems

Name _____

Section _____

Internet Exercises

4-1

_____

_____

_____

_____

4-2

_____

_____

_____

_____

_____

4-3

_____

_____

_____

_____

4-4

_____

_____

_____

_____

4-5

_____

_____

_____

_____

Chapter 5

Name ______________________________
Section __________

Question 1

Question 2

Question 3

Question 4

Question 5

Question 6

_____

_____

_____

_____

_____

Question 7

_____

_____

_____

_____

Question 8

_____

_____

_____

_____

Question 9

_____

_____

_____

Question 10

_____

_____

_____

_____

_____

_____

Question 11

_____

_____

_____

_____

Question 12

_____

_____

_____

_____

Question 13

_____

_____

_____

_____

Question 14

_____

_____

_____

Question 15

_____

_____

_____

Question 16

_____

_____

_____

Question 17

_____

_____

_____

_____

Question 18

_____

_____

_____

_____

Question 19

_____

_____

_____

_____

Question 20

_____

_____

_____

_____

Multiple choice: _____

1. _____	6. _____
2. _____	7. _____
3. _____	8. _____
4. _____	9. _____
5. _____	10. _____

SE5-1

a. _____

b. _____

c. _____

d. _____

e. _____

f. _____

g. _____

h. _____

SE5-2

_____

_____

_____

_____

_____

_____

SE5-3

General Journal	Debit	Credit

SE5-4

SE5-5

SE5-6

SE5-7

SE5-8

SE5-9

General Journal

Date	Accounts and Explanations	Post. Ref.	Debit	Credit

Name _____
Section _____

SE5-10

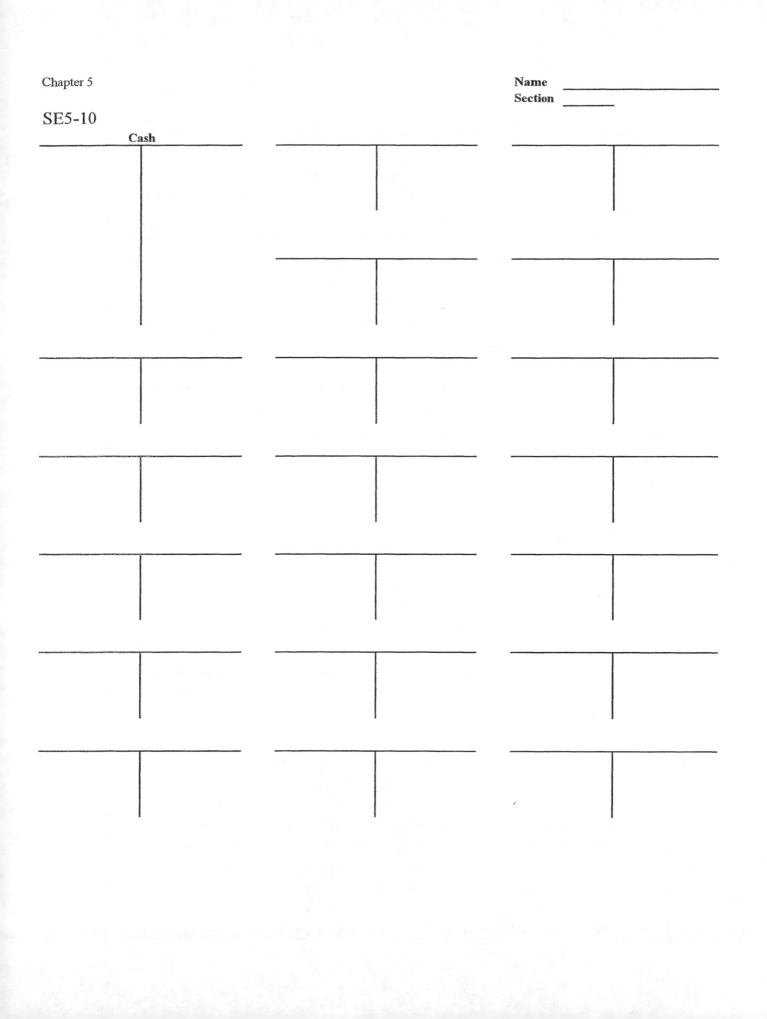

Cash

SE5-11

SE5-12

SE5-13

SE5-14

SE5-15

SE5-16

SE5-17

SE5-18

General Journal

Date	Accounts and Explanations	Post. Ref.	Debit	Credit

General Journal

Date	Accounts and Explanations	Post. Ref.	Debit	Credit
E5-1A				
E5-2A				
E5-3A				

E5-4A

_____

_____

_____

_____

_____

E5-5A

E5-6A

_____

_____

_____

_____

_____

_____

_____

_____

_____

_____

_____

_____

_____

_____

_____

E5-7A

General Journal

Date	Accounts and Explanations	Post. Ref.	Debit	Credit

Name _____

Section _____

E5-8A

General Journal

Date	Accounts and Explanations	Post. Ref.	Debit	Credit

Name _____
Section _____

E5-9A

Cash

E5-10A

E5-11A

E5-12A

E5-13A

E5-14A

E5-15A

E5-16A

E5-17A

General Journal

Date	Accounts and Explanations	Post. Ref.	Debit	Credit

E5-18A

_____
_____
_____
_____
_____
_____
_____
_____
_____
_____

E5-19A

_____
_____
_____
_____
_____
_____
_____
_____
_____
_____
_____

General Journal

Date	Accounts and Explanations	Post. Ref.	Debit	Credit
E5-1B				
E5-2B				
E5-3B				

E5-4B

_____

E5-5B

E5-6B

E5-7B

General Journal

Date	Accounts and Explanations	Post. Ref.	Debit	Credit

E5-8B

General Journal

Date	Accounts and Explanations	Post. Ref.	Debit	Credit

Name _____

Section _____

E5-9B

Cash

E5-10B

E5-11B

E5-12B

E5-13B

E5-14B

E5-15B

E5-16B

E5-17B

General Journal

Date	Accounts and Explanations	Post. Ref.	Debit	Credit

E5-18B

E5-19B

P5-1A

P5-2A

P5-3A

General Journal

Part a.

Date	Accounts and Explanations	Post. Ref.	Debit	Credit

Name _____

Section _____

P5-3A (continued)

General Journal

Part a.

Date	Accounts and Explanations	Post. Ref.	Debit	Credit

P5-3A (continued) Part b.

Cash		Inventory	

Part c.
_____
_____
_____
_____
_____
_____

Part e.
_____
_____
_____
_____
_____
_____
_____
_____
_____
_____

P5-3A (continued) Part d.

P5-4A

General Journal

Part a.

Date	Accounts and Explanations	Post. Ref.	Debit	Credit

P5-4A (continued) Part b.

Cash	Inventory	

Part c.

Part e.

P5-4A (continued) Part d.

P5-5A

General Journal

Part a.

Date	Accounts and Explanations	Post. Ref.	Debit	Credit

P5-5A (continued) Part b.

Cash	Inventory	

Part f.

P5-5A (continued) Part c.

Account	Debit	Credit

Part d.

Part e.

Name _____

Section _____

P5-6A

Part a.

Part b.

Part c.

P5-7A Part a.

Part b.

_____

_____

_____

_____

_____

_____

_____

_____

_____

_____

_____

_____

_____

_____

_____

_____

_____

_____

Name _____

Section _____

P5-8A

General Journal

Part a.

Date	Accounts and Explanations	Post. Ref.	Debit	Credit

P5-8A (continued) Part b.

Cash

Part c.

Part e.

P5-8A (continued) Part d.

P5-9A

General Journal

Part a.

Date	Accounts and Explanations	Post. Ref.	Debit	Credit

P5-9A (continued) Part b.

Cash

Part c. _____

_____

_____

_____

_____

_____

_____

Part e. _____

_____

_____

P5-9A (continued) Part d.

P5-10A

General Journal

Part a.

Date	Accounts and Explanations	Post. Ref.	Debit	Credit

P5-10A (continued) Part b.

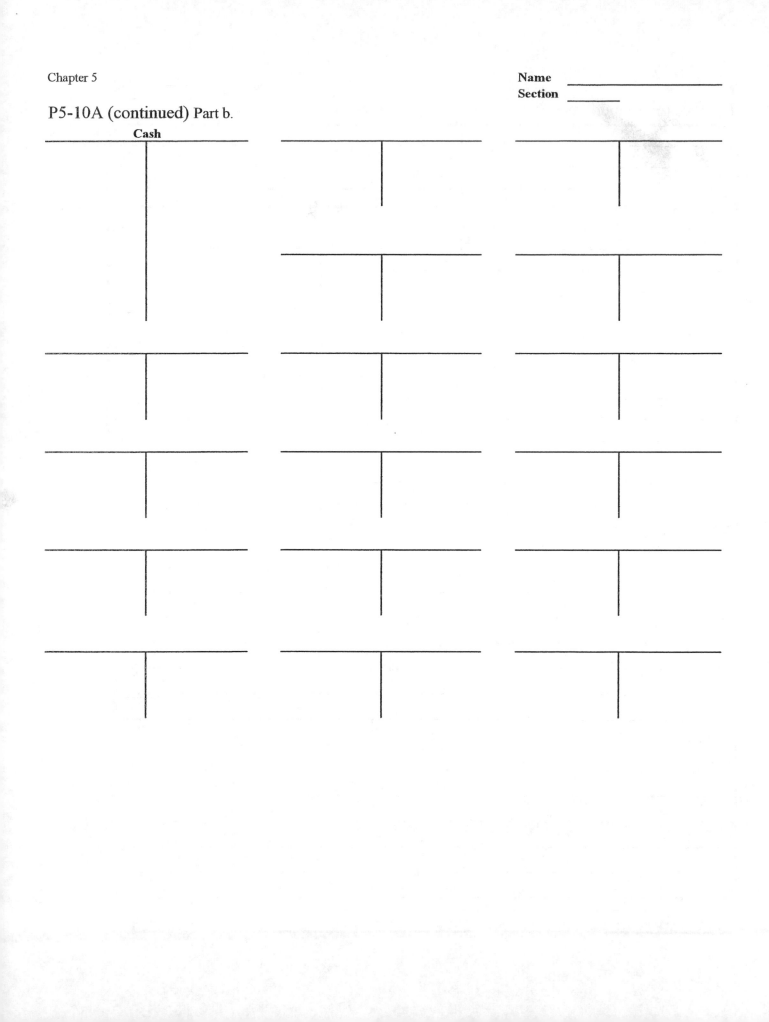

Cash

P5-10A (continued) Part c.

Account	Debit	Credit

Part d.

Part g.

P5-10A (continued) Part e.

Part f.

P5-1B

_____

_____

_____

_____

_____

_____

_____

_____

_____

_____

_____

_____

_____

P5-2B

_____

_____

_____

_____

_____

_____

_____

_____

_____

_____

_____

_____

_____

P5-3B

General Journal

Part a.

Date	Accounts and Explanations	Post. Ref.	Debit	Credit

Name _____

Section _____

P5-3B (continued)

General Journal

Part a.

Date	Accounts and Explanations	Post. Ref.	Debit	Credit

P5-3B (continued) Part b.

Cash			Inventory				

Part c.

_____

_____

_____

_____

_____

_____

Part e.

_____

_____

_____

_____

_____

_____

_____

_____

P5-3B (continued) Part d.

Name _____

Section _____

P5-4B

General Journal

Part a.

Date	Accounts and Explanations	Post. Ref.	Debit	Credit

P5-4B (continued) Part b.

Cash	Inventory	

Part c. _____

_____

_____

_____

_____

_____

Part e. _____

_____

_____

_____

_____

_____

_____

_____

_____

P5-4B (continued) Part d.

Name _____

Section _____

P5-5B

General Journal

Part a.

Date	Accounts and Explanations	Post. Ref.	Debit	Credit

P5-5B (continued) Part b.

Cash	Inventory	

Part f.

_____

_____

_____

_____

_____

_____

_____

_____

_____

_____

_____

_____

P5-5B (continued) Part c.

Account	**Debit**	**Credit**

Part d.

Part e.

P5-6B

Part a.

_____

_____

_____

_____

_____

_____

_____

_____

_____

Part b.

_____

_____

_____

_____

_____

_____

_____

_____

Part c.

_____

_____

_____

_____

_____

_____

_____

_____

_____

_____

_____

_____

P5-7B Part a.

Part b.

Name _____

Section _____

P5-8B

General Journal

Part a.

Date	Accounts and Explanations	Post. Ref.	Debit	Credit

P5-8B (continued) Part b.

Cash

Part c. _____

_____

_____

_____

_____

_____

_____

Part e. _____

_____

_____

P5-8B (continued) Part d.

P5-9B

General Journal

Part a.

Date	Accounts and Explanations	Post. Ref.	Debit	Credit

P5-9B (continued) Part b.

Cash

Part c. _____

_____

_____

_____

_____

_____

_____

Part e. _____

_____

_____

P5-9B (continued) Part d.

P5-10B

General Journal

Part a.

Date	Accounts and Explanations	Post. Ref.	Debit	Credit

P5-10B (continued) Part b.

Cash

P5-10B (continued) Part c.

Account	Debit	Credit

Part d.

_____

_____

_____

_____

_____

_____

_____

Part g.

_____

_____

_____

_____

_____

_____

_____

P5-10B (continued) Part e.

Part f.

Financial Statement Analysis Problems

5-1

5-2

5-3

Name _____

Section _____

Critical Thinking Problems

Group Assignment

Internet Exercises

5-1

_____

_____

_____

_____

5-2

_____

_____

_____

_____

_____

_____

_____

_____

_____

_____

_____

5-3

_____

_____

_____

_____

_____

_____

_____

_____

_____

Question 1

_____

_____

_____

_____

Question 2

_____

_____

_____

_____

Question 3

_____

_____

_____

_____

Question 4

_____

_____

_____

Question 5

_____

_____

_____

_____

_____

_____

Question 6

_____

_____

_____

_____

Question 7

_____

_____

_____

_____

Question 8

_____

_____

_____

_____

Question 9

_____

_____

_____

_____

Question 10

_____

_____

_____

_____

_____

_____

Question 11

_____

_____

_____

_____

_____

_____

Question 12

_____

_____

_____

_____

_____

_____

Multiple choice:

1. _____
2. _____
3. _____
4. _____
5. _____
6. _____
7. _____
8. _____
9. _____
10. _____

SE6-1

SE6-2

SE6-3

Name _____

Section _____

SE6-4

SE6-5

SE6-6

SE6-7

SE6-8

_____

_____

_____

_____

_____

SE6-9

_____

_____

_____

_____

SE6-10

_____

_____

_____

_____

SE6-11

_____

_____

_____

_____

_____

_____

_____

_____

_____

_____

_____

SE6-12

_____

_____

_____

SE6-13

a. _____

b. _____

c. _____

d. _____

SE6-14

_____

_____

_____

_____

_____

SE6-15

_____

_____

_____

_____

SE6-16

_____

_____

_____

_____

_____

_____

_____

_____

_____

_____

E6-1A

E6-2A

E6-3A

_____

_____

_____

_____

_____

_____

_____

_____

_____

_____

_____

_____

_____

_____

E6-4A

_____

_____

_____

_____

_____

_____

_____

_____

_____

_____

_____

_____

_____

_____

E6-5A

E6-6A

E6-7A

_____

_____

_____

_____

_____

_____

_____

_____

_____

E6-8A

a. _____

b. _____

E6-9A

_____

_____

E6-10A

a. _____

_____

_____

b. _____

_____

E6-11A

_____

_____

E6-12A

_____

_____

E6-13A

E6-14A

E6-15A

General Journal	Debit	Credit

E6-16A

General Journal	Debit	Credit

E6-17A

E6-18A

E6-19A

E6-1B

_____

_____

_____

_____

_____

_____

_____

_____

_____

E6-2B

_____

_____

_____

_____

_____

_____

_____

_____

_____

_____

_____

_____

_____

_____

_____

_____

_____

_____

E6-3B

_____

_____

_____

_____

_____

_____

_____

_____

_____

_____

_____

_____

_____

_____

E6-4B

_____

_____

_____

_____

_____

_____

_____

_____

_____

_____

_____

_____

_____

_____

_____

E6-5B

E6-6B

E6-7B

_____

_____

_____

_____

_____

_____

_____

_____

_____

E6-8B

a. _____

b. _____

E6-9B

_____

E6-10B

a. _____

_____

b. _____

_____

E6-11B

_____

_____

E6-12B

_____

_____

E6-13B

_____

_____

_____

_____

_____

_____

_____

_____

_____

_____

_____

_____

_____

_____

_____

_____

E6-14B

_____

_____

_____

_____

_____

_____

_____

_____

_____

_____

_____

_____

_____

_____

_____

_____

E6-15B

General Journal	Debit	Credit

E6-16B

General Journal	Debit	Credit

E6-17B

E6-18B

E6-19B

P6-1A Parts a,b,c,d

P6-2A Parts a,b,c,d,e,f,g,h

P6-3A Parts a,b,c

Name _____

Section _____

P6-4A Part a.

P6-4A (continued) Part b.

P6-4A (continued) Part b.

P6-4A (continued) Part b.

P6-4A (continued) Part b.

P6-4A (continued) Part b.

P6-4A (continued) Part b.

Name _____

Section _____

P6-4A (continued) Parts c,d,e

Name _____

Section _____

P6-5A Parts a,b,c

Name _____

Section _____

P6-6A

Chapter 6

Name ______________
Section ______________

P6-7A Part a.

Part b.

Part c.

Part d.

Part e.

Name _____

Section _____

P6-8A Parts a,b

Name _____

Section _____

P6-9A Parts a,b,c,d

_____

_____

_____

_____

_____

_____

_____

_____

_____

_____

_____

_____

_____

_____

_____

_____

_____

_____

_____

_____

_____

_____

_____

_____

_____

_____

_____

_____

_____

P6-10A Parts a,b,c

Name _____

Section _____

P6-11A Parts a,b,c

Name _____

Section _____

P6-12A Parts a,b

Name _____

Section _____

P6-1B Parts a,b,c,d

Name _____

Section _____

P6-2B Parts a,b,c,d,e,f,g,h

Name _____

Section _____

P6-3B Parts a,b,c

Name _____

Section _____

P6-4B Part a.

P6-4B (continued) Part b.

P6-4B (continued) Part b.

P6-4B (continued) Part b.

P6-4B (continued) Part b.

P6-4B (continued) Part b.

P6-4B (continued) Part b.

P6-5B Parts a,b,c

Name _____

Section _____

P6-6B

P6-7B Part a.

Part b. _____

Part c. _____

Part d. _____

Part e. _____

_____

_____

Name _____

Section _____

P6-8B Parts a,b

Name _____

Section _____

P6-9B Parts a,b,c

P6-10B Parts a,b,c

Name _____

Section _____

P6-11B Parts a,b,c

P6-12B Parts a,b

Financial Statement Analysis Problems

6-1

6-2

Name _____

Section _____

Critical Thinking Problems

Name _____

Section _____

Internet Exercises

Question 1

_____
_____
_____
_____
_____

Question 2

_____
_____
_____
_____

Question 3

_____
_____
_____
_____

Question 4

_____
_____
_____

Question 5

_____
_____
_____
_____
_____
_____

Question 6

Question 7

Question 8

Question 9

Question 10

Question 11

_____

_____

_____

_____

_____

Question 12

_____

_____

_____

_____

Question 13

_____

_____

_____

_____

Question 14

_____

_____

_____

_____

Question 15

_____

_____

_____

_____

_____

_____

_____

Question 16

_____

_____

_____

Question 17

_____

_____

_____

Question 18

_____

_____

_____

Question 19

_____

_____

_____

Multiple choice:

1. _____
2. _____
3. _____
4. _____
5. _____
6. _____
7. _____
8. _____
9. _____
10. _____

SE7-1

SE7-2

SE7-3

SE7-4

SE7-5

SE7-6

SE7-7

SE7-8

General Journal	Debit	Credit
a)		
b)		

SE7-9

_____

_____

_____

_____

_____

_____

_____

SE7-10	Balance per	Type of
Item	Books	adjustment
Outstanding checks		
Service charge by bank		
NSF check from customer		
Deposits in transit		
Error made by bank		
Note receivable collected by bank		

SE7-11	Balance per	Type of
Item	Books	adjustment
Outstanding checks		
Service charge by bank		
NSF check from customer		
Deposits in transit		
Error made by bank		
Note receivable collected by bank		

SE7-12

SE7-13

SE7-14

General Journal	Debit	Credit

SE7-15

E7-1A

_____

_____

_____

_____

_____

E7-2A Part a.

General Journal	Debit	Credit

Part b.

_____

_____

_____

Part c.

_____

_____

_____

E7-3A Part a. General Journal	Debit	Credit

Part b.

_____

_____

_____

_____

Part c.

_____

_____

_____

_____

E7-4A

_____

_____

_____

_____

_____

E7-5A

Part a.

_____

_____

_____

Part b.

_____

_____

_____

Part c.

_____

_____

_____

_____

E7-6A

General Journal	Debit	Credit

E7-7A

E7-8A

_____

_____

_____

_____

_____

_____

_____

_____

E7-9A

_____

_____

_____

_____

_____

_____

_____

_____

_____

_____

General Journal	Debit	Credit

Name _____

Section _____

E7-10A

_____

_____

_____

_____

_____

_____

_____

_____

E7-11A Part a.

_____

_____

_____

_____

Part b.

_____

_____

_____

_____

_____

_____

_____

_____

Part c. General Journal	Debit	Credit

Name _____

Section _____

E7-12A

E7-13A

E7-14A

Name _____
Section _____

E7-1B

_____

_____

_____

_____

_____

_____

E7-2B Part a.

General Journal	Debit	Credit

Part b.

_____

_____

_____

_____

Part c.

_____

_____

_____

_____

Name _____

Section _____

E7-3B Part a.

General Journal	Debit	Credit

Part b. _____

_____

_____

_____

Part c. _____

_____

_____

_____

E7-4B

_____

_____

_____

_____

E7-5B

Part a. _____

_____

_____

_____

Part b. _____

_____

_____

Part c. _____

_____

_____

_____

E7-6B

General Journal	Debit	Credit

E7-7B

E7-8B

E7-9B

General Journal	Debit	Credit

E7-10B

_____
_____
_____
_____
_____
_____
_____
_____
_____

E7-11B Part a.

_____
_____
_____
_____
_____

Part b.

_____
_____
_____
_____
_____
_____
_____
_____

Part c. General Journal	Debit	Credit

E7-12B

E7-13B

E7-14B

Name _____

Section _____

P7-1A

P7-2A

Name _____

Section _____

P7-3A

General Journal

Date	Accounts and Explanations	Post. Ref.	Debit	Credit

P7-3A (continued)

General Journal

Date	Accounts and Explanations	Post. Ref.	Debit	Credit

Name _____

Section _____

P7-4A

Name _____

Section _____

P7-5A Part a.

Part b. General Journal	Debit	Credit

P7-6A Part a.

Part b. General Journal	Debit	Credit

Name _____

Section _____

P7-7A

1. _____

2. _____

3. _____

4. _____

5. _____

P7-8A Part a.

_____

_____

_____

_____

_____

_____

_____

_____

Part b.

_____

_____

_____

_____

_____

Part c.

_____

_____

_____

_____

_____

_____

_____

P7-1B

P7-2B

Name _____

Section _____

P7-3B

General Journal

Date	Accounts and Explanations	Post. Ref.	Debit	Credit

P7-3B (continued)

General Journal

Date	Accounts and Explanations	Post. Ref.	Debit	Credit

P7-4B

P7-5B Part a.

Part b. General Journal	Debit	Credit

Name _____

Section _____

P7-6B Part a.

Part b.	General Journal	Debit	Credit

Financial Statement Analysis Problems (continued)

7-3

Name _____

Section _____

Critical Thinking Problems

Chapter 7

Internet Exercises

Name _____

Section _____

Question 1

_____

_____

_____

_____

_____

Question 2

_____

_____

_____

_____

Question 3

_____

_____

_____

_____

Question 4

_____

_____

_____

_____

Question 5

_____

_____

_____

_____

_____

_____

Question 6

Question 7

Question 8

Question 9

Question 10

Question 11

_____
_____
_____
_____

Question 12

_____
_____
_____
_____

Question 13

_____
_____
_____
_____

Question 14

_____
_____
_____
_____

Question 15

_____
_____
_____
_____
_____
_____

Question 16

_____

_____

_____

_____

_____

Question 17

_____

_____

_____

_____

Question 18

_____

_____

_____

_____

Question 19

_____

_____

_____

_____

Question 20

_____

_____

_____

_____

_____

_____

Question 21

_____

_____

_____

_____

_____

_____

_____

Multiple choice:

1. _____

2. _____

3. _____

4. _____

5. _____

6. _____

7. _____

8. _____

9. _____

10. _____

_____

_____

_____

_____

_____

_____

_____

SE8-1

SE8-2

SE8-3

SE8-4

_____

_____

_____

_____

_____

_____

_____

SE8-5

_____

_____

_____

_____

_____

_____

_____

SE8-6

_____

_____

_____

_____

_____

_____

_____

_____

_____

_____

_____

SE8-7

SE8-8

SE8-9

SE8-10

SE8-11

General Journal	Debit	Credit

_____

_____

_____

SE8-12

_____

_____

_____

SE8-13

_____

_____

SE8-14

_____

_____

SE8-15

a. _____

b. _____

c. _____

d. _____

e. _____

f. _____

g. _____

SE8-16

a. _____

b. _____

c. _____

d. _____

SE8-17

_____

_____

_____

_____

_____

_____

SE8-18

_____

_____

_____

SE8-19

_____

_____

_____

_____

SE8-20

_____

_____

_____

_____

_____

SE8-21

_____

_____

_____

_____

_____

SE8-22

_____

_____

_____

_____

_____

_____

SE8-23

_____

_____

_____

_____

SE8-24

_____

_____

_____

_____

_____

_____

_____

_____

_____

_____

_____

_____

_____

E8-1A Parts a,b,c

_____

_____

_____

_____

_____

_____

_____

_____

_____

_____

E8-2A Parts a,b,c,d — General Journal	Debit	Credit

_____

_____

_____

_____

_____

_____

_____

_____

_____

_____

_____

E8-3A Parts a,b,c

General Journal	Debit	Credit

E8-4A Parts a,b,c

Name _____

Section _____

E8-5A Parts a,b,c

_____

_____

_____

_____

_____

_____

_____

_____

_____

E8-6A

_____

_____

_____

E8-7A Parts a,b,c

_____

_____

_____

_____

_____

_____

_____

_____

_____

_____

_____

_____

_____

Name _____

Section _____

E8-8A Parts a,b,c

General Journal	Debit	Credit

_____

_____

_____

_____

_____

_____

_____

_____

_____

_____

_____

_____

E8-9A

General Journal	Debit	Credit

E8-10A

General Journal	Debit	Credit

E8-11A

_____

_____

_____

_____

E8-12A

a. _____

b. _____

c. _____

d. _____

e. _____

f. _____

g. _____

h. _____

i. _____

j. _____

E8-13A Parts a,b,c

E8-14A Parts a,b,c,d

General Journal	Debit	Credit

E8-15A Parts a,b.

E8-16A Parts a,b

E8-17A Parts a,b,c,d

Name _____

Section _____

E8-18A Parts a,b,c,d

General Journal	Debit	Credit

E8-19A

E8-20A

a.

b.

c.

d.

e.

f.

E8-21A Parts a,b

_____

_____

_____

_____

_____

_____

_____

_____

E8-22A

_____

_____

_____

_____

_____

_____

_____

_____

_____

_____

_____

_____

_____

_____

_____

_____

_____

_____

_____

Name _____

Section _____

E8-1B Parts a,b,c

_____

_____

_____

_____

_____

_____

_____

_____

_____

_____

_____

E8-2B Parts a,b,c,d — General Journal	Debit	Credit

_____

_____

_____

_____

_____

_____

_____

_____

_____

_____

_____

E8-3B Parts a,b,c   General Journal   Debit   Credit

	Debit	Credit

_____

_____

_____

_____

_____

_____

_____

E8-4B Parts a,b,c

_____

_____

_____

_____

_____

_____

_____

_____

_____

_____

_____

_____

_____

_____

_____

_____

Name _____

Section _____

E8-5B, Parts a,b,c

_____

_____

_____

_____

_____

_____

_____

_____

_____

E8-6B

_____

_____

_____

E8-7B Parts a,b,c

_____

_____

_____

_____

_____

_____

_____

_____

_____

_____

_____

_____

_____

E8-8B Parts a,b,c

General Journal	Debit	Credit

_____

_____

_____

_____

_____

_____

_____

_____

_____

_____

E8-9B

_____

_____

_____

_____

E8-10B

General Journal	Debit	Credit

E8-11B

_____

_____

_____

_____

E8-12B

a. _____

b. _____

c. _____

d. _____

e. _____

f. _____

g. _____

h. _____

i. _____

j. _____

E8-13B Parts a,b,c

_____

_____

_____

_____

_____

_____

_____

_____

_____

_____

_____

_____

_____

_____

_____

_____

_____

_____

_____

Name _____

Section _____

E8-14B Parts a,b,c,d   General Journal   Debit   Credit

General Journal	Debit	Credit

E8-15B Parts a,b.

E8-16B Parts a,b

_____

_____

_____

_____

_____

_____

_____

_____

_____

_____

E8-17B Parts a,b,c,d

_____

_____

_____

_____

_____

_____

_____

_____

_____

_____

_____

_____

_____

_____

_____

_____

_____

_____

_____

_____

E8-18B Parts a,b,c,d

General Journal	Debit	Credit

E8-19B

E8-20B

a.

b.

c.

d.

e.

f.

E8-21B Parts a,b

_____

_____

_____

_____

_____

_____

_____

_____

E8-22B

_____

_____

_____

_____

_____

_____

_____

_____

_____

_____

_____

_____

_____

_____

_____

_____

_____

_____

Name _____

Section _____

P8-1A Parts a,b

P8-2A Part a

1. Straight-line method

Year	Rate	Beginning Book Value	Annual Depreciation	Accum. Depr.	Ending Book Value
2007					
2008					
2009					
2010					

2. Double-declining balance method

Year	Rate	Book Value	Annual Depreciation	Accum. Depr.	Ending Book Value
2007					
2008					
2009					
2010					

3. Activity method

Year	Rate	Book Value	Annual Depreciation	Accum. Depr.	Ending Book Value
2007					
2008					
2009					
2010					

Part b.

P8-5A

General Journal	Debit	Credit

Name _____

Section _____

P8-6A

General Journal	Debit	Credit

P8-7A

Name _____

Section _____

P8-8A

P8-9A Part a

1. Straight-line method

Year	Rate	Beginning Book Value	Annual Depreciation	Accum. Depr.	Ending Book Value
2007					
2008					

2. Double-declining balance method

Year	Rate	Book Value	Annual Depreciation	Accum. Depr.	Ending Book Value
2007					
2008					

Part b.

P8-10A Part a.

General Journal	Debit	Credit

_____
_____
_____
_____
_____
_____

Part b.

General Journal	Debit	Credit

_____
_____
_____
_____
_____
_____

Part c.

_____
_____
_____
_____
_____
_____
_____
_____
_____
_____
_____

P8-1B Parts a,b

P8-2B Part a

1. Straight-line method

Year	Rate	Beginning Book Value	Annual Depreciation	Accum. Depr.	Ending Book Value
2007					
2008					
2009					
2010					

2. Double-declining balance method

Year	Rate	Book Value	Annual Depreciation	Accum. Depr.	Ending Book Value
2007					
2008					
2009					
2010					

3. Activity method

Year	Rate	Book Value	Annual Depreciation	Accum. Depr.	Ending Book Value
2007					
2008					
2009					
2010					

Parts b,c

_____

_____

_____

_____

_____

_____

_____

_____

_____

_____

_____

_____

_____

P8-3B Part a

1. Straight-line method

Year	Rate	Book Value	Annual Depreciation	Accum. Depr.	Ending Book Value
2007					
2008					
2009					
2010					
2011					

2. Double-declining balance method

Year	Rate	Book Value	Annual Depreciation	Accum. Depr.	Ending Book Value
2007					
2008					
2009					
2010					
2011					

Part b.

Part c.

Name _____

Section _____

P8-4B Parts a,b,c

1. Straight-line method

	Year	Rate	Beginning Book Value	Annual Depreciation	Accum. Depr.	Ending Book Value
	2006					
	2007					
	2008					
	2009					
	2010					

2. Activity method

	Year	Rate	Book Value	Annual Depreciation	Accum. Depr.	Ending Book Value
	2006					
	2007					
	2008					
	2009					
	2010					

3. Double-declining balance method

	Year	Rate	Book Value	Annual Depreciation	Accum. Depr.	Ending Book Value
	2006					
	2007					
	2008					
	2009					
	2010					

Name _____

Section _____

P8-5B

General Journal	Debit	Credit

Name _____

Section _____

P8-6B

General Journal	Debit	Credit

Name _____

Section _____

P8-7B

Name _____

Section _____

P8-8B

P8-9B Part a

1. Straight-line method

Year	Rate	Beginning Book Value	Annual Depreciation	Accum. Depr.	Ending Book Value
2007					
2008					

2. Double-declining balance method

Year	Rate	Book Value	Annual Depreciation	Accum. Depr.	Ending Book Value
2007					
2008					

Part b.

Name _____
Section _____

Critical Thinking Problems

_____
_____
_____
_____
_____
_____
_____
_____
_____
_____

_____
_____
_____
_____
_____
_____
_____
_____
_____
_____
_____
_____
_____
_____
_____
_____

Name _____
Section _____

P8-10B Part a.

General Journal	Debit	Credit

_____
_____
_____
_____
_____

Part b.

General Journal	Debit	Credit

_____
_____
_____
_____

Part c.

_____
_____
_____
_____
_____
_____
_____
_____

Financial Statement Analysis Problems

_____

_____

_____

_____

_____

_____

_____

_____

_____

_____

_____

_____

_____

_____

_____

_____

_____

_____

_____

_____

_____

_____

_____

_____

_____

_____

_____

_____

_____

_____

Internet Exercises

_____

_____

_____

_____

_____

_____

_____

_____

_____

_____

_____

_____

_____

_____

_____

_____

_____

_____

_____

_____

_____

_____

_____

_____

_____

_____

_____

_____

Name _____

Section _____

Question 1

_____

_____

_____

_____

_____

Question 2

_____

_____

_____

_____

Question 3

_____

_____

_____

_____

Question 4

_____

_____

_____

Question 5

_____

_____

_____

_____

_____

_____

_____

Question 6

_____

_____

_____

_____

_____

Question 7

_____

_____

_____

_____

_____

Question 8

_____

_____

_____

_____

_____

Question 9

_____

_____

_____

_____

Question 10

_____

_____

_____

_____

_____

_____

_____

Question 11

_____
_____
_____
_____

Question 12

_____
_____
_____
_____

Question 13

_____
_____
_____
_____

Question 14

_____
_____
_____
_____

Question 15

_____
_____
_____
_____
_____
_____

Question 16

_____

_____

_____

_____

Question 17

_____

_____

_____

_____

Question 18

_____

_____

_____

_____

Question 19

_____

_____

_____

_____

Multiple choice:

1. _____
2. _____
3. _____
4. _____
5. _____
6. _____
7. _____
8. _____
9. _____
10. _____

SE9-1

Accounts payable

Unearned revenue

Warranty payable

SE9-2

a.

b.

c.

d.

e.

SE9-3

SE9-4

General Journal	Debit	Credit

SE9-5

_____

_____

_____

_____

SE9-6

_____

_____

_____

_____

SE9-7

_____

_____

_____

SE9-8

_____

_____

_____

SE9-9

_____

_____

_____

SE9-10

_____

_____

_____

_____

SE9-11

SE9-12

SE9-13

SE9-14

SE9-15

a.

b.

c.

SE9-16

a.

b.

c.

SE9-17

_____
_____
_____
_____
_____
_____

SE9-18

_____
_____
_____
_____
_____
_____

SE9-19

_____
_____
_____
_____
_____
_____

SE9-20

_____
_____
_____
_____
_____
_____

E9-1A _____

a. _____

b. _____

c. _____

d. _____

e. _____

E9-2A Parts a,b,c _____

_____

_____

_____

E9-3A — General Journal	Debit	Credit

E9-4A Parts a,b,c — General Journal	Debit	Credit

_____

_____

_____

_____

_____

E9-5A Parts a,b,c,d

_____

_____

_____

_____

_____

_____

_____

_____

E9-6A Parts a,b

_____

_____

_____

_____

_____

_____

_____

_____

_____

_____

_____

E9-7A

General Journal	Debit	Credit

Name _____
Section _____

E9-8A Parts a,b,c,d   General Journal   Debit   Credit

	Debit	Credit

E9-9A Parts a,b,c

_____

_____

_____

_____

_____

_____

E9-10A Parts a,b,c

_____

_____

_____

_____

E9-11A Parts a,b,c   General Journal   Debit   Credit

	Debit	Credit

E9-1B

a. _____

b. _____

c. _____

d. _____

e. _____

E9-2B Parts a,b,c

_____

_____

_____

_____

E9-3B

General Journal	Debit	Credit

E9-4B Parts a,b,c

General Journal	Debit	Credit

_____

_____

_____

_____

_____

E9-5B Parts a,b,c,d

_____

_____

_____

_____

_____

_____

_____

_____

_____

E9-6B Parts a,b

_____

_____

_____

_____

_____

_____

_____

_____

_____

_____

_____

E9-7B

General Journal	Debit	Credit

Name _____

Section _____

E9-8B Parts a,b,c,d | General Journal | Debit | Credit

General Journal	Debit	Credit

E9-9B Parts a,b,c

E9-10B Parts a,b,c

E9-11B Parts a,b,c | General Journal | Debit | Credit

General Journal	Debit	Credit

E9-12B Parts a,b,c

_____
_____
_____
_____
_____
_____

E9-13B Parts a,b,c

_____
_____
_____
_____
_____

E9-14B Parts a,b,c

_____
_____
_____
_____
_____

E9-15B

_____
_____
_____
_____

E9-16B

_____
_____
_____
_____
_____

E9-17B

_____

_____

_____

_____

_____

E9-18B

a. _____

b. _____

c. _____

d. _____

e. _____

E9-19B Parts a,b,c

General Journal	Debit	Credit

E9-20B Parts a,b,c

General Journal	Debit	Credit

Name _____

Section _____

P9-1A Parts a,b,c

General Journal	Debit	Credit

P9-2A Parts a,b,c,d

P9-3A Parts a,b,c,d

P9-4A Part a

Loan 1	Year	Cash Payment	Interest	Principal reduction	Principal balance
	1				
	2				
	3				
	4				

Loan 2	Year	Cash Payment	Interest	Principal reduction	Principal balance
	1				
	2				
	3				
	4				

Part b.

Part c.

Name _____

Section _____

P9-5A

General Journal	Debit	Credit

P9-6A Parts a,b,c,d

_____

_____

_____

_____

_____

_____

_____

_____

_____

_____

_____

P9-7A Parts a,b,c,d

_____

_____

_____

_____

_____

_____

_____

_____

P9-8A Parts a,b,c,d

_____

_____

_____

_____

_____

_____

_____

_____

_____

_____

_____

_____

_____

_____

_____

_____

_____

_____

_____

_____

_____

_____

_____

Name _____

Section _____

P9-1B Parts a,b,c

General Journal	Debit	Credit

Name _____

Section _____

P9-2B Parts a,b,c,d

_____

_____

_____

_____

_____

_____

_____

_____

_____

_____

_____

_____

P9-3B Parts a,b,c,d

_____

_____

_____

_____

_____

_____

_____

_____

_____

_____

_____

_____

_____

_____

_____

P9-4B Part a

Loan 1

	Year	Cash Payment	Interest	Principal reduction	Principal balance
	1				
	2				
	3				
	4				

Loan 2

	Year	Cash Payment	Interest	Principal reduction	Principal balance
	1				
	2				
	3				
	4				

Part b.

_____
_____
_____
_____
_____
_____
_____

Part c.

_____
_____
_____
_____
_____
_____
_____
_____
_____
_____

P9-5B

General Journal	Debit	Credit

P9-6B Parts a,b,c

_____

_____

_____

_____

_____

_____

_____

_____

_____

_____

_____

_____

Critical Thinking Problems

Name _____

Section _____

Internet Exercises

Name _____

Section _____

Question 1

_____

_____

_____

_____

Question 2

_____

_____

_____

_____

Question 3

_____

_____

_____

_____

Question 4

_____

_____

_____

_____

Question 5

_____

_____

_____

_____

_____

_____

Question 6

_____

_____

_____

_____

Question 7

_____

_____

_____

_____

Question 8

_____

_____

_____

_____

Question 9

_____

_____

_____

Question 10

_____

_____

_____

_____

_____

_____

SE10-1

SE10-2

SE10-3

General Journal	Debit	Credit

SE10-4

SE10-5

SE10-6

SE10-7

_____

_____

_____

_____

SE10-8

_____

_____

_____

SE10-9

_____

_____

_____

SE10-10

_____

_____

_____

SE10-11

_____

_____

_____

SE10-12 General Journal	Debit	Credit

SE10-13 General Journal	Debit	Credit

SE10-14

SE10-15

SE10-16

SE10-17

SE10-18

SE10-19

SE10-20

Name _____
Section _____

E10-1A

_____

_____

_____

_____

_____

E10-2A Parts a,b

_____

_____

_____

_____

E10-3A

General Journal	Debit	Credit

E10-4A

_____

_____

_____

_____

E10-5A

a. _____

b. _____

c. _____

E10-6A

_____

_____

_____

_____

E10-7A Parts a,b,c,d,e

_____

_____

_____

_____

_____

_____

_____

_____

_____

_____

_____

_____

_____

Name _____

Section _____

E10-8A

	General Journal	Debit	Credit

E10-9A

Name _____

Section _____

E10-10A

Common Stock

Additional Paid-in Capital

Retained Earnings

Treasury Stock

E10-11A Parts a,b,c,d,e

Name _____

Section _____

E10-12A   General Journal   Debit   Credit

	Debit	Credit

E10-13A

E10-14A

E10-15A

_____

_____

_____

_____

_____

E10-16A

	Assets	Liabilities	SH Equity	Equity section affected
Issued shares at par				
Issued shares above par				
Declared cash dividend				
Paid cash dividend				
Purchased treasury stock				
Sold treasury shares for cost				
Distributed stock dividend				
Announced stock split				
Issued preferred stock above par				

E10-17A

_____

_____

_____

_____

_____

_____

_____

_____

_____

_____

_____

_____

Chapter 10

Name ____________________

Section ________

E10-1B

E10-2B Parts a,b

E10-3B General Journal	Debit	Credit

E10-4B

E10-5B

a.

b.

c.

E10-6B

E10-7B Parts a,b,c,d,e

Name _____

Section _____

E10-8B

General Journal	Debit	Credit

E10-9B

E10-10B

Common Stock

Paid-in Capital

Retained Earnings

Treasury Stock

E10-11B Parts a,b,c,d,e

Name _____

Section _____

E10-12B	General Journal	Debit	Credit

E10-13B

E10-14B

E10-15B

_____

_____

_____

_____

_____

E10-16B

	Assets	Liabilities	SH Equity	Equity section affected
Issued shares at par				
Issued shares above par				
Declared cash dividend				
Paid cash dividend				
Purchased treasury stock				
Sold treasury shares for cost				
Distributed stock dividend				
Announced stock split				
Issued preferred stock above par				

E10-17B

_____

_____

_____

_____

_____

_____

_____

_____

_____

_____

_____

_____

Name _____

Section _____

P10-1A Part a

General Journal	Debit	Credit

Part b.

_____

_____

_____

_____

_____

_____

_____

Part c.

Name _____

Section _____

P10-4A Part a

General Journal	Debit	Credit

Part b.

_____

_____

_____

_____

_____

Part c.

Part d.

_____

_____

_____

_____

P10-5A

P10-6A Parts a,b,c,d

Name _____

Section _____

P10-7A Parts a,b,c,d

P10-8A Parts a,b,c,d,e

Name _____

Section _____

P10-1B Part a

General Journal	Debit	Credit

Part b.

_____

_____

_____

_____

_____

_____

_____

Part c.

Name _____

Section _____

P10-2B Part a

General Journal	Debit	Credit

Part b.

_____

_____

_____

_____

_____

Part c.

_____

_____

_____

_____

_____

_____

_____

_____

_____

_____

_____

_____

_____

_____

_____

_____

_____

_____

_____

Name _____

Section _____

P10-3B Part a

General Journal	Debit	Credit

Part b.

_____

_____

_____

_____

_____

_____

_____

Part c.

Name _____

Section _____

P10-4B Part a	General Journal	Debit	Credit

Part b. _____

_____

_____

_____

_____

Part c.

Part d. _____

_____

_____

_____

P10-5B

P10-6B Parts a,b,c,d

_____

_____

_____

_____

_____

_____

_____

_____

_____

_____

_____

_____

_____

_____

_____

_____

_____

_____

_____

P10-7B Parts a,b,c,d

_____

_____

_____

_____

_____

_____

_____

_____

_____

_____

_____

P10-8B Parts a,b,c,d,e

_____

_____

_____

_____

_____

_____

_____

_____

_____

_____

_____

_____

_____

_____

_____

_____

_____

Name _____

Section _____

Financial Statement Analysis Problems

Question 1

_____

_____

_____

_____

_____

Question 2

_____

_____

_____

_____

_____

Question 3

_____

_____

_____

_____

Question 4

_____

_____

_____

Question 5

_____

_____

_____

_____

_____

_____

Question 6

_____

_____

_____

_____

_____

Question 7

_____

_____

_____

_____

_____

Question 8

_____

_____

_____

_____

_____

Question 9

_____

_____

_____

_____

_____

Question 10

_____

_____

_____

_____

_____

_____

_____

Question 11

_____
_____
_____
_____
_____

Question 12

_____
_____
_____
_____

Question 13

_____
_____
_____
_____

Question 14

_____
_____
_____
_____

Question 15

_____
_____
_____
_____
_____
_____

Name _____
Section _____

Question 16

_____
_____
_____
_____

Question 17

_____
_____
_____

Question 18

_____
_____
_____
_____
_____
_____

Multiple choice:

1. _____
2. _____
3. _____
4. _____
5. _____
6. _____
7. _____
8. _____
9. _____
10. _____

SE11-1

a. _____

b. _____

c. _____

d. _____

e. _____

SE11-2

a. _____

b. _____

c. _____

d. _____

e. _____

SE11-3

_____

_____

_____

_____

_____

SE11-4

_____

_____

_____

_____

_____

SE11-5

_____

_____

_____

_____

_____

SE11-6

_____

_____

_____

_____

SE11-7

_____

_____

_____

_____

SE11-8

_____

_____

_____

_____

SE11-9

_____

_____

_____

_____

SE11-10

_____

_____

_____

_____

_____

_____

SE11-11

_____

_____

_____

_____

SE11-12

_____

_____

_____

_____

SE11-13

_____

_____

_____

_____

SE11-14

_____

_____

_____

_____

SE11-15

_____

_____

_____

_____

_____

_____

SE11-16

_____

_____

_____

_____

_____

SE11-17

_____

_____

_____

_____

_____

SE11-18

_____

_____

_____

_____

SE11-19

_____

_____

_____

_____

_____

_____

_____

_____

_____

_____

_____

_____

E11-1A

	Inflows/outflows	Section of statement
a.		
b.		
c.		
d.		
e.		
f.		
g.		
h.		
i.		
j.		
k.		

E11-2A

	Amount	Inflows/outflows	Section of statement
a.			
b.			
c.			
d.			
e.			
f.			
g.			
h.			

Name _____

Section _____

E11-3A

E11-4A

E11-5A

E11-6A

a.

b.

c.

d.

E11-7A

E11-8A

E11-9A

a.

b.

c.

E11-10A

E11-11A

E11-12A

E11-13A

E11-14A

Name _____
Section _____

E11-15A

_____

_____

_____

_____

_____

E11-16A

_____

_____

_____

_____

_____

E11-17A

_____

_____

_____

_____

E11-18A

_____

_____

_____

_____

E11-19A

_____

_____

_____

_____

_____

E11-1B

	Inflows/outflows	Section of statement
a.		
b.		
c.		
d.		
e.		
f.		
g.		
h.		
i.		
j.		
k.		

E11-2B	Amount	Inflows/outflows	Section of statement
a.			
b.			
c.			
d.			
e.			
f.			
g.			
h.			

E11-3B

E11-4B

E11-5B

Name _____

Section _____

E11-6B

a. _____

_____

_____

b. _____

_____

_____

c. _____

_____

_____

d. _____

_____

E11-7B

_____

_____

_____

_____

E11-8B

_____

_____

_____

_____

E11-9B

a. _____

_____

_____

b. _____

_____

_____

c. _____

_____

E11-10B

_____

_____

_____

_____

_____

_____

_____

_____

_____

E11-11B

_____

_____

_____

_____

_____

_____

_____

_____

_____

E11-12B

_____

_____

_____

_____

_____

_____

_____

_____

E11-13B

_____

_____

_____

_____

_____

_____

_____

_____

_____

E11-14B

E11-15B

E11-16B

E11-17B

E11-18B

E11-19B

Name _____

Section _____

P11-1A Part a.

P11-1A Part a. (continued)

Parts b,c,d		

P11-2A Parts a,b,c

P11-3A

P11-4A

P11-5A

P11-6A Parts a,b

P11-7A Parts a,b

P11-8A Parts a,b

_____

_____

_____

_____

_____

_____

_____

_____

_____

P11-9A Parts a,b,c,d,e

_____

_____

_____

_____

_____

_____

_____

_____

_____

_____

_____

_____

_____

_____

_____

_____

_____

_____

Name _____

Section _____

P11-1B Part a.

P11-1B Part a. (continued)

Parts b,c,d		

P11-2B Parts a,b,c

_____
_____
_____
_____
_____
_____
_____
_____
_____

P11-3B

_____
_____
_____
_____
_____
_____
_____
_____
_____

P11-4B

_____
_____
_____
_____
_____
_____
_____
_____
_____
_____
_____

P11-5B

_____

_____

_____

_____

_____

_____

_____

_____

_____

P11-6B Parts a,b

_____

_____

_____

_____

_____

_____

_____

_____

P11-7B Parts a,b

_____

_____

_____

_____

_____

_____

_____

_____

_____

_____

_____

P11-8B Parts a,b

P11-9B Parts a,b,c,d,e

Name _____

Section _____

Financial Statement Analysis Problems

Name _____

Section _____

Critical Thinking Problems

Chapter 11

Internet Exercises

Question 1

_____

_____

_____

_____

_____

Question 2

_____

_____

_____

_____

_____

Question 3

_____

_____

_____

_____

_____

Question 4

_____

_____

_____

_____

Question 5

_____

_____

_____

_____

_____

_____

_____

Question 6

_____

_____

_____

_____

_____

Question 7

_____

_____

_____

_____

Question 8

_____

_____

_____

_____

Question 9

_____

_____

_____

_____

Question 10

_____

_____

_____

_____

_____

_____

_____

Multiple choice:

1. _____

2. _____

3. _____

4. _____

5. _____

6. _____

7. _____

8. _____

9. _____

10. _____

SE12-1

SE12-2

SE12-3

SE12-4

SE12-5

_____

_____

_____

_____

_____

_____

_____

_____

_____

SE12-6

_____

_____

_____

_____

_____

_____

_____

_____

SE12-7

_____

_____

_____

_____

_____

_____

_____

_____

_____

SE12-8

SE12-9

SE12-10

SE12-11

SE12-12 Parts a,b

SE12-13

SE12-14

SE12-15

SE12-16

E12-1A

_____

_____

_____

_____

_____

_____

_____

E12-2A

_____

_____

_____

_____

E12-3A

	2008	2007	2006	2005	2004
Sales	30000	28400	26300	24200	25400

_____

_____

E12-4A

_____

_____

_____

_____

_____

_____

_____

_____

_____

_____

_____

_____

Chapter 12

Name ______________________________

Section __________

E12-5A

E12-6A

E12-7A Parts a,b,c,d,e

E12-8A Parts a,b,c,d,e,f

E12-9A Parts a,b,c

E12-10A

E12-11A

E12-12A Parts a,b,c,d,e

E12-13A Parts a,b,c,d,e

E12-14A

_____

_____

_____

_____

_____

_____

_____

_____

_____

E12-15A

_____

_____

_____

_____

_____

_____

_____

_____

_____

_____

E12-16A General Journal	Debit	Credit

_____

_____

_____

_____

_____

_____

E12-1B

_____

_____

_____

_____

_____

_____

_____

E12-2B

_____

_____

_____

_____

E12-3B

	2010	2009	2008	2007	2006
Sales	27925	30400	33525	26250	30300

_____

_____

E12-4B

_____

_____

_____

_____

_____

_____

_____

_____

_____

_____

_____

_____

_____

Name ____________________________

Section _________

E12-5B

E12-6B

E12-7B Parts a,b,c,d,e

Chapter 12

Name ______________________

Section ________

E12-8B Parts a,b,c,d,e,f

E12-9B Parts a,b,c

Name _____

Section _____

E12-10B

Name _____

Section _____

E12-11B

E12-12B Parts a,b,c

E12-13B Parts a,b,c,d,e

E12-14B

_____

_____

_____

_____

_____

_____

_____

E12-15B

_____

_____

_____

_____

_____

_____

_____

_____

_____

E12-16B General Journal	Debit	Credit

_____

_____

_____

_____

_____

Name _____

Section _____

P12-1A Parts a,b,c

P12-2A

P12-3A Part a.

Part b.		

P12-4A Part a.

_____

_____

_____

_____

_____

_____

_____

_____

_____

_____

_____

_____

_____

_____

_____

_____

Part b.

_____

_____

_____

_____

_____

_____

_____

_____

_____

_____

_____

_____

_____

_____

Name _____

Section _____

P12-5A Part a.

_____

_____

_____

_____

_____

_____

_____

_____

_____

_____

_____

_____

_____

_____

_____

Part b.

_____

_____

_____

_____

_____

_____

_____

_____

_____

_____

_____

_____

_____

P12-6A Parts a,b

P12-7A Parts a,b

P12-8A Parts a,b

P12-1B Parts a,b,c

Name _____

Section _____

P12-2B

Name _____

Section _____

P12-3B Part a.

Part b.		

P12-4B Part a.

_____

_____

_____

_____

_____

_____

_____

_____

_____

_____

_____

_____

_____

_____

Part b.

_____

_____

_____

_____

_____

_____

_____

_____

_____

_____

_____

_____

_____

Name _____

Section _____

P12-5B Part a.

Name ____________________

Section ________

P12-6B Parts a,b

P12-7B Parts a,b,c

Name _____

Section _____

P12-8B Parts a,b

Name _____

Section _____

Critical Thinking Problems

Chapter 12

Internet Exercises

Question 1

_____

_____

_____

_____

_____

Question 2

_____

_____

_____

_____

Question 3

_____

_____

_____

_____

Question 4

_____

_____

_____

_____

Question 5

_____

_____

_____

_____

_____

_____

Question 6

_____
_____
_____
_____
_____

Question 7

_____
_____
_____
_____

Question 8

_____
_____
_____
_____

Question 9

_____
_____
_____
_____

Question 10

_____
_____
_____
_____
_____
_____

Question 11

_____

_____

_____

_____

_____

_____

Question 12

_____

_____

_____

_____

_____

_____

Question 13

_____

_____

_____

_____

_____

_____

Multiple choice:

1. _____
2. _____
3. _____
4. _____
5. _____

Name _____

Section _____

SE13-1

SE13-2

SE13-3

SE13-4

SE13-5

_____

_____

_____

_____

_____

_____

_____

SE13-6

_____

_____

_____

_____

_____

_____

_____

SE13-7

_____

_____

_____

_____

_____

_____

SE13-8

_____

_____

_____

_____

_____

_____

_____

SE13-9

_____

_____

_____

_____

_____

_____

SE13-10

_____

_____

_____

_____

_____

_____

SE13-11

_____

_____

_____

_____

_____

_____

_____

_____

_____

_____

_____

_____

_____

Name _____

Section _____

Internet Exercises